HOLY STUFF OF LIFE

HOLY STUFF OF LIFE

STORIES, POEMS, AND PRAYERS ABOUT HUMAN THINGS

Heather Murray Elkins

THE PILGRIM PRESS

CLEVELAND

T O Daniel, who makes a difference.

The Pilgrim Press, 700 Prospect Avenue, Cleveland, Ohio 44115-1100
thepilgrimpress.com

© Heather Murray Elkins
All rights reserved. Published 2006

Printed in the United States of America on acid-free paper
10   09   08   5   4   3   2

Library of Congress Cataloging-in-Publication Data

Elkins, Heather Murray.
    The holy stuff of life : stories, poems, and prayers about human things /
Heather Murray Elkins.
        p. cm.
    Includes bibliographical references and index.
    ISBN 0-8298-1723-9 (alk. paper)
    1. Meditations.   I. Title.
BV4832.3.E45 2006
242—dc22   2006001187

ISBN 13 : 978-0-8298-1723-2
ISBN 10 : 0-8298-1723-9

Stuff:

material to work with or upon, substance to be wrought,
matter of composition

what a person is "made of," one's capabilities or inward character

the materials, stores, or supplies belonging to an army

the kind of material used in a trade such as carpentry, "quarter stuff"

matter of an unspecified kind

articles of food or drink: the good stuff, cultivated produce
of a garden or farm

to gorge, to cram,

hoax, humbug a person

worthless ideas, discourse, or writing; nonsense, rubbish

to get "stuffed" — an expression of contempt/defiance

used to denote any collection of things about which one
is not able or willing to particularize

slang word for dust

to do one's stuff, to do what is required or expected of one

to know one's stuff, to be knowledgeable in one's subject

contents

acknowledgments

To acknowledge someone is to recognize that one's presence, to grant access, to honor that person's relationship with you. To acknowledge someone is to admit that you are in his or her debt.

With this in mind I acknowledge:

William Shakespeare for reminding us: "We are such stuff as dreams are made of, and our little lives are rounded by a sleep."

Adrienne Rich's poem "Transcendental Etude."

Laura Flippen Tenzel: a wise woman of holy stuff.

Wallace Stevens' notion of the poet's "instinct for earth."

Nancy Rosebaugh for teaching me to bless the simple things.

William Wesley, my partner, my friend, teacher and dream-maker.

And Uli Guthrie, an editor who certainly knows her stuff.

introduction

This book is a narrative treasure hunt for the implicit holiness of human things, a quest for a transformative encounter that turns consumption into consecration. On these pages you can explore the holy human connections of things such as apple seeds, a tattoo, dish towels, a broken chalice, a carpenter's level, and extra virgin cooking oil blessed by a pope. Here is a collection of stories, poems, and prayers about holy, human "stuff."

Human consciousness is a process of binding things together. We have a genetic disposition to "grasp" life and make tangible connections with the embodied language of our senses and our bodily and psychological relationships with things.

These "bound together" relationships are also the neural pathways for sacramental consciousness. What are these ties that bind? They are the verbal processing of sensed experience, ritual gestures, and the work of creating mental and material relationships. This process of binding, this consciousness of tangible connections is at the center of our ceremonial life (from the Latin, *caerimonia*, to bind back together that which is separate).

My fascination with the quiddity of life (the quality that makes a thing exactly what it is), requires me to explore a way of being human. Tattoos, shells, spoons, and brooms are those things that signify our creativity, family identity, life cycles, love, death, economics, and sexuality. Put more simply, "We are stuff,"[1] and this is a book for people who want to unpack what that sentence means.

In real life we have complex psychological relationships to things. We own, we treasure, we wonder at, we're protected by, and we're known by. Or we no longer own, we covet, we're suffocated by, allergic to, get the willies from. Between people and things lie infinite gradations of relationship. Our histories ready us as readers—our histories are, in fact, histories of our tenancy in the universe of stuff.[2]

My main intention in this book is to name and create consciousness of stuff or things as that reality which really matters. This universe of stuff offers us a process of altar-ing our selves and our world. To altar/alter is to lift up the common place of life for holy use. It is not simply an exercise or process that one experiences briefly, or only intellectually acknowledges. It is a transformative encounter between the holy and the human, an encounter that demands an entirely new way of being, "an attitude that sets us against the social set-up of our time."[3] I find myself in good company with scholars of material culture and poets who have long insisted on the implicit holiness of human things.

I've had a long-standing fascination with stuff. It may be more of an addiction than a fascination. I watch my mother slowly lose her grip on the difference between trash and treasure and know I'm seeing my own dilemma. Telling stories about things, however, is one way to resist objectification and struggle against amnesia. A lifelong discipline of asking "How do these things come into being?" may help as well. What meaning, memory, or sacred purpose can be grasped by these things? How can we learn to lay hands on spoons or brooms for the purpose of binding individual lives together in a tangible, experiential, sensual, and spiritual community of wholly holy humans?[4]

Feminist studies of the consequence of objects and the codes of meaning that they carry in the lives of women provide another handle on the topic of things. They reveal that "objects have different symbolic meanings for men and women, and hence, objects affect one's sense of agency in different ways."[5]

This difference can be also seen in cultures such as those in Appalachia that maintain identity through oral traditions rather than written language. The codes of authority as well as resistance are carried in stories, jokes, and songs.[6] It helps you to travel lightly, and cope with being on the margins. Writing these stories of human stuff and holy things was, for me, like making a page of patchwork out of pieces of skin. I wonder if I'll feel the cold more or less now that they can sit on a shelf.

An object that acquires symbolic voice in public discourse is more parable than plain speech. It requires a community of interpreters, those who can recite its story of origin, the tale of how it came to be a holy or profane presence in their midst[7]. In the beginning, however, there's a human who encounters a thing, an object, the inanimate stuff of life and hears something, something that's calling his or her name.

one   THINGS THAT SAY GRACE

T his is a book of fundamental things. These stories, prayers, and poems deal with the basic stuff of life such as eating and table manners. To remember and to say grace are two ways that humans make the act of eating something more than mere survival. This is the grammar of blessing that is at the center of the table prayers of all the children of Abraham.

The basic stuff of life, food and drink, can be a means of grace when we remember and give thanks, *eucharistein*. But sometimes we need to be reminded of our table manners by making room for the stranger, by feeding others as we've been fed, by remembering to bless the hand that serves the table. These are stories of things that taught me how to say grace.

Acts of God and Other Mysteries[1]

LIGHTENING: *Making or becoming lighter in weight.*
Reducing the weight or load of.

LIGHTNING: *A flash of bright light produced by an electric*
discharge between clouds or between clouds and the ground.

—Oxford Modern English Dictionary

ASHES TO ASHES. The farmhouse is gone.

The heart-jolting news zaps the phone lines, strikes my inner ear, and keeps traveling. I'm not well grounded. The last four years of my life are piled like fallen leaves around my feet. I'm frantically stuffing my accumulation of higher education into two trunks and one backpack so I won't be late for graduation.

This is not a good time for bad news. I should have remembered that spring is our family's season of high drama, packed with graphic scenes of near death, real destruction, minor catastrophes, and major miracles. I should be grateful that my family's alive, even though they'll miss my graduation.

The shock is wearing off. I lean against the wall for support and listen to a tale of old wiring, a missing lightning rod, little rain, and an act of God. The farmhouse is gone. In less than an hour, five generations of the artifacts of our lives have gone up in smoke. Story-shaped things begin to drift through my mind like ash in the wind as I listen to Mother's voice. The walnut staircase that my aunt floated down on her way to the parlor to marry a man who called her Baby Doll. The cherry wood bed set that fired a thirty-year feud. A kitchen table scarred from the knives of hired men who used them for everything from killing pigs to eating peas. A homemade pie safe with star-shaped vent holes and oak shelves stained by tart berry juice. A porch swing whose squeak signaled sundown and triggered the whip-poor-will.

"Get ready," my mother says. I hold the dorm phone and wonder how one gets ready for an act of God. We'd survived our exile in the Arizona desert for twenty-five years, going from one summer's watering hole to the next. The farmhouse on Spring Creek was the sacred center of our universe, the lode stone that drew us together on a yearly pilgrimage to Almost Heaven West Virginia. Whatever the word "home" means just went up in smoke.

> The pilgrimage is a spiritual quest for a change, a transformation of oneself and relief from profound suffering, distress, anguish and illness. The pilgrimage begins as a response to a crisis. It may begin with a crisis of personal disintegration. It may be motivated by the remembrance of a lost integrity and by the hope of regaining it. The pilgrimage implies the refusal to accept the present condition of confusion and suffering as final; it implies that conviction that there is a way of transcending this condition, despite all the evidence to the contrary.[2]

I hang up the phone, pack my possessions, and try to get ready. By sundown, I've added a diploma to my backpack and I'm driving due east. The one-car caravan includes just me, Mother, and my youngest sister. The others will follow our trail.

We've been raised on exodus rations, knowing, as an old song goes, "This world is not our home. We're just a' passin' through." Palestine, West—by God—Virginia is the holy land, the place we came from, and therefore to which ontologically we belong. We're in exile whenever we're elsewhere. We're chronically displaced persons. It's probably the reason we not only picked up hitchhikers but also took them home for supper. We understood the ancient prayer of homesick Jews and the restlessness of migrant workers. You dream about home when you don't want to, and whenever you can.

This summer of endings, this season of shaking foundations may be a blessing in disguise, a chance to rest in peace. Questions get louder as we drive in the direction of the sunrise. Is it time to give up the ghost of the family farm? To turn over the deed, write "paid in full," and give it back to Mother Nature? The insurance payment will barely keep us fed for the summer since Palestine is "in the country" where the lightning acts of God don't amount to much in the way of hard cash.

"We must make a list," Mother says, "of what we've lost." She names each object like it's a child, wraps it up with its story string still intact, and writes its name on whatever paper comes within reach. I have my own way of counting, seeing things as clearly then as now. We travel toward the place of their destruction, yet they are as real as any sacramental presence can be.

    A top-of-the-line table saw
    A box of leather-bound books
    A name-bearing Bible
    A silver cross with a sky-blue stone
    An apron from France
    A large looking glass that reflected more than two dimensions
    A new generator
    An old-fashioned washtub with claw feet
    New tools, some with unstained handles

We reach the stone foundation two-and-a-half days later. Two-and-a-half days of straight driving fueled by arguments, storytelling, and songs for the road. That's how it's done. Since the radio rarely works in the assorted vehicles we drive, our oral tradition is strengthened, preserved on such road trips. It will be years before I realize that, except for the shaped-note hymns, every song we know is from the 1920s. "Oh! We ain't got a barrel of money. Maybe we're ragged and funny . . ."

It's late afternoon. I turn left at the Blue Goose, last stop for gas/groceries/gossip. I sound the horn at all the blind curves, a sure sign that the driver is not from around here, or grew up driving buggies around the mountains. I slow the car on the last curve as I've been taught: Stop. Look across the valley. There's a hole in the horizon and a faint gray haze that could be early evening fog. The pre–Civil War farmhouse, three stories high, is gone. All that's left is a smoky pillar that held the fireplaces, and the foundation is filled with twisted pieces of the past.

I park the car under the oak that once shaded a porch, get out and circle the scorched stones. *Ashes to ashes, we all fall down.* I find myself humming. I hum when I'm nervous. *We all fall down.*

My youngest sister, Tamara, quietly watches from the shelter of the car. My mother inspects the rotting remains of the smokehouse, a structure that I regret to say was spared from the flames.

The shadows are growing as the sun declines. I turn to the car trunk, deciding to assert a little order. I assume I'll find a tent, or a canvas, bedrolls, and some means of cooking. We've driven nonstop, and it never occurs to me that we've set out unprepared. I expect to find the bare necessities. I find foolishness instead: an antique lace tablecloth, the odds and ends of family china, mismatched silver, a glass lamp, a McGuffy's Reader, and some of her mother's heirlooms that migrated with us when we first traveled west. This is more chaos than I can manage. I go from speechless to loud incoherence. Where in heaven's name do we sleep? What on earth do we eat or work with? We need tools, not treasure. No tent. No matches. No common sense . . .

"Don't worry," Mother says. "I called the neighbors when we stopped for gas in town."

Her assurance turns me speechless again. Now there is nothing left to do but kick cans, or whatever the scorched remains once were. Years of stockpiled possibilities, shelves, closets, attics filled with plans for our homecoming have been struck like lightning, by lightning. All our attempts to inherit a life are pathetically scattered, scorched beyond recognition, exposed in plain sight. Ashes to ashes. We all fall down. Chaos and non-sense is the hardest part of dying. Chaos unnerves every meaning and mocks every attempt of structure, any hope of sanity.

I return to the scorched heap and start digging. I'm on a mission impossible, trying to read the rubbish as if it's braille. I'm searching for a sign. Somewhere in this ruin is or was the silver cross with a stone of the bluest blue, like a tear distilled a hundred thousand times. In my rational mind, I know the iron bolts on the windows melted like wax, yet I keep searching for a cross made of silver.

I saw the cross first at a Camp Farthest Out, It was—and still might be—an organization of tongues-speaking, dream-interpreting Christians founded in the years before Pentecostals joined Fortune 500 and were invited to the White House for breakfast and prayer. I was thirteen, searching for spaces where women's voices had weight and public shape. Whatever else might have been missing in this camped out community, they did take the book of Joel to heart and in practice. The Holy Spirit poured out through many female shapes and sounds, but it is the image of a man that I remember. It hovers over the foundation as I dig.

He is a Palestinian Christian, a double alien to us. He depends on the kindness of these Pentecostal strangers. He is a jeweler, just as his father's fathers had been. He's a storyteller in exile, separated from a holy land because of . . . and here what I hear unravels my innocence that is also ignorance. I only recognize one chosen people, only one holy book, only one holy land. I hear another story, a Christian story, from someone born in Palestine, who has seen children of Abraham exiled, abandoned, and left to die. He tells a dangerously different story from the one we know as he works silver magic with his hands weaving a story and a cross.[3]

He and his extended family had forty-eight hours to pack for an exodus that turned into an exile in hell. He took his tools, his stones, his silver, his father, his wife, and his two sons and carried them into a nowhere. Once a people, now no people, had a land, now no land, and both are bordered with barbed wire. He speaks softly, but his words strike like lightning, The Promised Land hadn't been empty. I know I've never heard this story before. It will be years before I hear this again. He thanks us for helping him, for hearing him. He asks us to pray for a family he hadn't seen in years as he works to bring them home, wherever that might be.

The year of his exile is the year I was born, 1948. I watch him work the true blue stone into the cross's center. It is, he says, the color of a Palestine sky. I want that cross. I covet that vision of silver and blue. It costs too much, I know, but Mother wants it as well. Nothing will get between her and that story-shaped thing. So, at meeting's end, one month of our grocery money goes to support exiles from Palestine. Whatever we have to eat for the rest of that month is flavored with my father's irritation and the beauty of that cross.

I track that cross like a human metal detector through our countless moves from house to house. I learn to pay attention to a few treasures and their stories, keeping track of their location, knowing they could get lost in the cracks, left behind in the whirlwinds of our migrations.

I'd seen it last in the left-hand drawer of the walnut sideboard in the parlor of the farmhouse. This was the marrying/burying parlor whose plaster cracks had been transformed by my mother's artfulness into painted ivy. Green veined leaves of Wandering Jew crept along the walls and up the corner where they spread to frame the tin-foiled moon that masked a missing piece of the ceiling.

I'd considered stealing it at the summer's end. I spent a long time looking at it in the drawer. Mother had brought it to Palestine as part of a Bible school presentation. We weren't allowed to wear it. Bearing the cross, she'd say, not wearing. As we prepared to head west into the sunset, I worried about leaving it behind. The new young tenants promised to leave the parlor untouched. This parlor was to be the first stage in Mother's plan for an old-fashioned country museum. She'd filled it with artifacts and family fictions. A Palestinian cross for Palestine, West Virginia. But surely this was too beautiful and terrible to leave behind. Only the threat of scripture held me back. He was crucified with thieves, I'd been told. I left it in the drawer.

I wish I'd succumbed to temptation. The new tenants manage to escape the holocaust with their lives and most of their belongings in the twenty minutes it takes to incinerate the foundation. I wish they'd taken it. It's intolerable that nothing is spared, nothing is saved; nothing remains.

I dig with a broken hoe blade that I found in the smokehouse. I know it's pointless, but I keep digging. The longer I dig, the more frantic I feel. I spend over an hour shifting through the rubble by hand looking for some remnant of melted silver, searching for a blackened blue stone. I dig as if I think something living is under the rubble, praying to be rescued.

. . .

I REMEMBER THIS SENSATION years later when I watch firefighters dig with their bare hands in gray ash of September 11, 2001, desperately seeking for any signs of life. I see images of Israeli mothers trying to find flesh of their flesh in blown up buses and restaurants. I read news of Palestinians being buried alive under bulldozed homes. The terror of history is its repetition. I dig in the smoky ruins of this memory as if I could unearth a breathing life. I imagine voices: "We are people here!" Is there any holy ground, any human reason buried under the rubble? Is there a place where the unholy wars of faction and fact are laid to rest? The more I dig the louder the distortions; the facts and artifacts have been bulldozed beyond recognition, blown to bits, buried in the rubble and the footnotes.

. . .

I stop digging up the past when an electrical company truck pulls into the lane and parks. The man who emerges looks more than a little lost. That's normal, given the pattern of our public lives. He looks at me, covered with ashes, my mother who is spreading a lace tablecloth on the grass, and my car-sitting sister. He ventures a little closer, clears his throat and asks in a cautious way, "When . . . when did this happen?"

I'm irrationally angry at his question and spit out an answer. "Three weeks ago!" *Mad as spit is very mad indeed.* "Can we *help* you?" "Well," he says, "well, I came to read the meter." He looks at me and then at the three floors of smoky trash I'm standing on. "Well," he says, "well, I'm supposed to read the meter."

My face assumes what my sisters call a stone-cold snake glare. I invite him, by all means, to read the meter if he can find it. I abandon him to the ash pit and my mother's cheerful inquisition about his family, faith, and future. I cross the meadow, heading for the barn.

This field has seen human generations struggle against principalities and power, in mortal combat with entropy. The uncut hay lacks the smell of human sweat and crushed clover. I pass the rusted sickle, the baling twine unraveling. I hear echoes of my grandfather's World War I service song in the crows, his voice loud and joyfully off-key: "How you gonna keep 'em down on the farm, after they've seen Paree?"

I reach the barn, relieved to see its lopsided door propped open. Perhaps we can bed down here for the night. It won't be the first time this structure has sheltered a human species. Our family is used to the notion of "barning." One step inside and I'm assaulted by a swarm of would-be killer bees. Three stings to the face and I resemble Quasimodo. My lips are sticking further out than my nose by the time I beat a retreat back to the foundation.

Mother has the electric company man well in hand until he gets sight of my distorted appearance. My sister's eyes go round and she gets out of the car, so I know it's bad. I retreat to the shade just in time to see another utility truck arrive. This time it's the phone company, and the man who climbs out is clearly more confused than our first visitor. He has trouble making eye contact. I don't blame him; I can barely see and I've started to drool. Mother starts explaining about the Depression and how her parents bought this farm but then we had to move to Arizona because I'm sick (and what he thinks I suffer from I can't imagine) but we're going to come back, but now lightning . . . and all the while the meter man is trying to read a hunk of melted steel. The phone man starts backing toward his truck.

"Don't mind him," I say. "He's trying to read the meter. Can I help you?"

"Are you," he asks in a very neutral tone, still avoiding my eyes, "the woman who called about a phone from Parkersburg?"

My mother abandons her story about God, debts, and the Depression and jumps in with the answer. "Oh yes," she says, "I'm the one who called. Let's get you started."

Confused he may be, but not stupid. He looks at the ramshackle shed, the foundation, the lopsided barn across the meadow, the foundation again, the surrounding landscape empty of human structures, and cautiously asks, "Excuse me, Ma'am, where exactly do you want me to put the phone?"

"Here," Mother says, and points to the large oak singed on the side that faced a missing porch. "On the tree. We'll be camping out, you see, and I can't do without a phone."

To his credit, he ignores the odd sound that the meter man makes and backs up to his truck. He makes his company phone call, keeping his eyes and his questions politely neutral. Oddly enough it turns out that there is no company policy that exactly forbids putting phones on trees. It doesn't say it can't be done. No one had ever asked.

What happens next could have come from a sense of the ridiculous, or the disorientation that most rule-abiding folk experience when they're exposed to Mother for any length of time. It might have been compassion. It's a mystery to me. In no time at all, these two men install the world's first tree phone. They even go so far as to build a little roof to keep the rain off the line. Mother invites them to supper.

She tells us to set the table, which means a lace cloth spread on the grass with mismatched spoons and saucers. Of course there's no supper, but we set the table anyway. My sister is practicing her Buddhist detachment. I try to not panic, reminding myself of the little boy and Jesus, even though in that story somebody had enough common sense to pack a lunch.

The light grows longer, dropping down on the hills. I sit on the smoky stones. Perhaps we'll pretend to have tea. Who needs sympathy or tents, or houses, or meals on wheels?

Then just as the sun settles, I see the neighbors. They are "comin' roun' the mountain." Neighbors with tents and jelly, corn and ham, homemade bread and chocolate cake.

Behold, I show you a mystery: lace tablecloths spread on the grass, phones on the tree. Human community requires communion and communication, but at its heart is the mysterious hospitality of God. What makes for peace in Palestine or west-by-God-anywhere? A table in the presence of our neighbors and our enemies? Pray that the lightening strikes soon.

The Life of a Spoon

In its beginning and to its end, human life requires feeding. Somebody had to feed us or we wouldn't be here. To be spoon fed is a sign of vulnerability; we are either too young or too infirm to feed ourselves, yet it is also a revelation of relationship. To stretch out a spoon is to extend a table of hospitality in God's name and for Christ's sake.

This spoon work requires remembering how we've been fed and blessing the hands that have fed us. Memorial and thanksgiving form the centerpiece of sacramental fellowship. We help, however, in setting the table. We need reminders of how to say grace.

I have a spoon. It's not my baby spoon—God knows where that's gone after a lifetime of moving. I hope it's still in circulation in some Goodwill universe. What I have is a silver Korean spoon. My father brought it home from the war. It came with a set of chop sticks, but they vanished somewhere along the trail of our family's endless migration from house to house and east to west.

He never told us why he brought home a set of silverware. It seemed odd for a war trophy. He got medals, but we never saw them. He did show us a picture of two children, a girl of seven and her brother who was younger. He told us about finding these children, or how they found him.

The United States and South Korean forces were being forced south of Seoul. He was with the Army Corps of Engineers and their job was to build roads for the retreating officers and equipment and to stand in between to slow the Chinese advance. The children found him at a stream, shaving. They were dirty and starving. He offered the girl part of his rations, a comb, and a piece of soap and thought he'd seen the last of them. She returned, her brother in hand, and they were washed, combed, and smiling. He let them stay, fed them, taught them a little English, and learned a little Korean. He wrote home about adopting them and sent us the picture. He tried to keep them with his unit when they had to retreat but was ordered to leave them behind. He paid a family to feed them. He lost the children but kept the story and the silverware.

I grow up wondering about these missing members of our family tree. I study their picture and finger the spoon. When the chopsticks are lost, I hide the spoon in the box of things I keep under whatever bed I'm in. The picture and spoon get imprinted on my synapses, deepening the connections over the years.

I start digging for the story of the spoon when I find myself with the power of a pen as the academic dean of a seminary that sent the first Methodist missionary, Henry Appenzeller, to the Land of Morning Calm. My father's razor and the spoon sit on the shelf above my desk. There are excellent academic reasons to establish a faculty exchange program between Drew and Ewha Women's University in South Korea. It's the largest women's university in the world, and its first president was Alice Appenzeller, daughter of that first Drew graduate. I stare at the spoon on my shelf and think that it's time to follow it home.

Perhaps I hope to heal the memory of a missing sister or discover the reason my father kept a spoon. I need to know the rest of the story.

I write a grant; I give up the front office and travel to South Korea to teach liturgical theology at Ewha. It's not what I expected. It's not what anyone expected. Two weeks after I arrive, September 11, 2001, explodes the world as we know it. All the systems of communication—phone, e-mail, airlines—go down.

Two weeks later the phones work again and I get a call from Bill, my husband. He's coming to Korea as soon as the airports open and he's bringing my father. I'm so desperately grateful that I don't question the wisdom of bringing a failing veteran back to a war zone. They arrive one week after airports have reopened. I meet them at the airport and watch my husband hold my father's arm as he sets foot on Korean soil again, fifty-one years later. They arrive on the day we declare war on terrorism by bombing Afghanistan. I know why my husband's come. I don't know what's gotten into my father. He's eighty-three years old, and his legs are giving out, his eyes failing. When I ask why he's come he simply says he wants to see a people who'd been "to hell and back again" before he dies.

We take him to see bridges and roads and city streets. We go to the Monument for Peace that overlooks the DMZ, a place where a war of half a century is still being waged. He stands and looks at the Bridge of Freedom in silence. I finally ask him about the silverware, to explain the spoon. He answers me without looking, "It's the weapon of a Christian."

The answer explodes my hard-line assumptions about why he wears a veteran's cap that says "Korea" and what sense he's made of his life as an Appalachian faithfully serving his country in two world wars. A spoon is the weapon of a Christian. It is a powerful weapon, an instrument of peace, a source of love and power, a means to Christ's end: feed my lambs. To use the power of spoons is to employ every skill we possess as peacemakers at the table in the household of God.

> In dealing with the humanity of the sacraments we have to take very seriously what humans perceive as well as what God does. And this is not merely a matter of the intellect but the perception of the senses—all the senses. Sacramentality, then, is basically taking seriously our full humanity.[4]

In its beginning and at its end, human life requires feeding, and human life lived in *imago Christi* requires that we begin by saying grace. I pack the spoon for a Korean Thanksgiving service to be held in a small Methodist church by the Eastern Sea. It is located on the top of a hill overlooking the last civic structure in South Korea, a lighthouse. The beam from that lighthouse shines directly into the church's windows. I've prepared a sermon on Thanksgiving, *eucharistia*, saying grace.

I discover the sermon has arrived before me. The words, "Give thanks" are written in Korean and placed on the wall above the preachers' chairs. A community feast is going to follow the service to celebrate the first visit the church has ever had from seminary faculty. My translator and mentor is Dr. Se Hyoung Lee, one of our alumni from Drew. The Thanksgiving liturgical design is very beautiful. A wooden stand that is used like a backpack by vendors is holding a rainbow of vegetables and fruit. There are clusters of red peppers, kimchi pots, drying herbs. The Korean word for "give thanks" is displayed like a fine painting, and mounted at the front of the sanctuary.

It's going to be a service of spoons. I've learned something about traditional Korean spoons over the last three months. In traditional Korean culture one has a lifelong relationship with a spoon. If it's given as a gift to a child, it's a small size. When the child grows, the mother takes the spoon to a metal worker and has the spoon handle extended, so it grows just like the child. Korean spoons, even contemporary ones, have a more intimate connection in a person's life than most North Americans experience.

I've asked the pastor to invite all the members of the congregation to bring their spoons when they come to church this Sunday. Everyone arrives, spoon in hand. They are mystified by the pastor's request, but they've done what he asked. "What are the spoons for?" they ask at the door. Every one wants to know about the spoons. I say it's a mystery. The men laugh. They like this.

I have a simple sermon, as simple as a spoon. I'm going to show them my father's spoon, tell them the mystery of its travels, then close with a story about Thanksgiving. I plan to ask them to remember how they've been spoon-fed by God and those who love them. I ask them to consider what it means when Jesus tells us, "Feed my lambs." I'll remind them of what they know better than I do, that there are children and elders starving less than twenty miles away, separated from them by barbed wire and half a century of war. I plan to say grace at the end and ask for a blessing on our spoons.

I start with a question: How do we learn to bless the hand that feeds us? How do we learn to say, "Thank you," when we're in the wilderness, or on the thirty-eighth parallel? Who teaches us to bless, not bite the hand that feeds us? Who teaches them how to use spoons?

I learned the secret of a spoon at my mother's mother's table. At the age of a hundred and six, she'd moved from feeding to being fed. I've framed her final lesson in my memory. My older sister's kitchen is filled with the noisy sounds and wonderful smells of a multigenerational Thanksgiving dinner. My oldest sister inherited our grandmother's cooking skills; I inherited the ability to boil water. I did as I was told: feed Grandma. Long after other tastes have departed, the sense of bitter and sweet remains, so Grandma eats desert first. I spoon-feed her ice cream, my attention elsewhere, until she stops the spoon. Being blind, she traces the spoon to my fingers, and kisses my hand.

It's a simple gesture of gratitude and a profound sacramental insight. To kiss the hand that feeds you is eucharist, thanksgiving to feed others as you have been fed is eucharist, thankful giving. I tell them the story of my grandmother's spoon and its sacramental teaching. I show them my father's spoon. I tell them its story and the power it holds: "This is the weapon of a Christian."

When I look at their faces, I know they know what it means. These are those who have family on the other side of the line that they haven't seen for more than half a century. These are those who stand guard at the edge of no man's land, a required service for every young man in a country divided in its body and soul. These are those who voluntarily maintain a road in this village that no one has been permitted to travel for over fifty years. Members of this congregation work to keep the road open on their side of the line; they pray it will someday be the highway of peace.

It's a last-minute decision to ask for a basket so that they can bring their spoons forward and offer them up for prayer. The handmade food warmer, *pab sang po*, that they've given me I use to line the basket.

I invite them to remember; I invite them to say grace; I invite them to come forward and place their spoons in a basket as a sign that they are willing to use these spoons in the work of peace. I invite them to be willing to feed the lambs as Jesus asked regardless of which side of the line they're on. I call them to bring their spoons to Christ's table as a sign they are willing to do the unthinkable—share a table with their enemies.

Old men, women, children, have all brought their "own" spoons. Spoons: the weapons of Christians. I stand beside the pastor. We wait. They come, each carrying a spoon like a treasure: young, old, men, women, and children. One young mother walks forward, holding her spoon firmly in one hand, her baby against her heart with the other. She puts her spoon in the basket and then takes her baby's bottle and places it in the basket beside her spoon. She tells the pastor that she wants her child to be fed with the gospel.

I pray, and the pastor starts to pray, then breaks down, fighting tears, trying to finish. There's a long unnatural silence, and I hear an odd rattling sound. I risk a look. He's standing there, holding the basket above his head. His hands are trembling. What I'm hearing is the sound of the spoons. After a long pause he sighs, says a brief sentence, and puts the basket back on the altar. We are all puzzled, trying not to stare. He's had a vision, I'm told later, a vision of spoons. When he'd lifted the basket, he heard a voice say: "There are only 141 spoons here. Where are the other two thousand?" The voice repeated the question again and fell silent.

I ask Dr. Lee to ask the pastor what he thinks it means. The answer is that he doesn't know, but he and his people will pray until they find out, and when they find out, they will start working with their spoons. What he trusts is that God has called this church to a witness uniquely their own. A vision of spoons, weapons of Christians on the front lines of war.

> We declare to you what was from the beginning, what we have heard, what we have seen with our eyes, what we have looked at and touched with our hands, . . . we declare to you.
> (1 John 1:1–3)

I read the headlines about the threat of weapons of mass destruction and peace delegations. I study the curved artifact that rests on my desk. I wonder about the work of silverware; I'm looking for the evidence of spoons.

Stirring Women

We are stirred by a sense
    as common as spoons.
    Amen.

We are capable
    of cupping God.
    So be it.

We believe in the destiny of dining.
We ladle grace like gravy
    over the bread of life.

In a hard-to-handle time
    we are good at getting to the bottom,
    gripped in Necessity's hand.

We invent perpetual motion
    from a rounded shape
    and a hungry sound.

Few if any
    are born to the taste of silver.
Most acquire stainless steel.

We inspect tear spots
    and expect tarnish.
We polish tea spoons
    and offer sympathy
    with just a trace of acid.

Let others sharpen their wits,
  pare away distinctions,
  separate the jointedness of time.

We are spoon-fed, start to finish.
Stir, lift, and blend mercy
  served warm.

Let us be good and godly as spoons.
  Amen.[5]

Recipes for a Love Feast

THE LOVE FEAST IS A REENACTMENT of the early Christian meal found in John 13. This "agape" meal communicated fellowship in Christ, joyful witness, and mutual service. It is an ecumenical means of sharing at table when the sacrament of communion is not possible. The leadership of this service is open to all those who have been baptized. It is a service that typically takes place in informal settings. The food should be clearly distinct from Eucharistic bread. Almonds, cranberries, chocolate, or rice crackers can be easily shared.

The following prayers can be used with singing, scripture, a sermon, or sharing stories of faith, hope, and love.

A FEAST OF LOVE

LEADER: This is a table for breaking the fast that comes from sorrow.
This is a place where there's "plenty good room."
This is a space where Love is in charge of the guest list
And reservations aren't required.

ALL: Breakfast is ready and the Son has risen.

LEADER: So, come, come just as you are,
You who have all the hope you need
And you who keep running out,
You who have only questions,
And you who have only one answer.

ALL: Breakfast is ready and the Son has risen.

LEADER: So, come, come just as you can,
You who have been here forever,
And you who've gone missing a very long time.

ALL: **Breakfast is ready and the Son has risen.**

LEADER: So, come, come just as God made you,
You have nothing to offer that isn't God's own.
Pull up a chair; the grace is amazing,
Makes a body feel at home.

ALL: **Breakfast is ready and the Son has risen.**

LEADER: Let us pray:

ALL: **Make us bread.**
Knead us well.
Help us rise.

LEADER: For bacon, eggs, and buttered toast,
Praise Father, Son, and Holy Ghost.

ALL: **Make us bread.**
Knead us well.
Help us rise.

LEADER: For bagels, beans, and chili roast,
Praise Mother, Child, and heavenly Hosts.

ALL: **Make us bread.**
Knead us well.
Help us rise.[6]

Ask people to gather themselves into "households" of three or four. One member from each group will come forward and bring back food for their household in a common bowl. Each one of the household should have the time to share a brief story of holy human dining. Each shares his or her answer to the question, "What food do I eat when I want to feel loved?" When all are finished with their answers, everyone replies: "Welcome Home."

Rags of Suffering, Robes of Joy

CLOTH AND CLOTHING ARE AMONG the most ancient cultural artifacts of the human species. The biblical account of Genesis 3:21 depicts God as the first "clothier" of creation. "And the LORD God made garments of skins for the man and for his wife, and clothed them."

From this scriptural dressing to the fashion page in this week's Sunday paper, humanity has been "into" clothes. We are born naked, but that is not our natural social attire. A complete absence of clothing indicates a lack of social responsibility in nearly every culture. Cloth in combination with behavior defines humanity.

Not surprisingly, clothing provides identifying marks for both individuals and societies. Clothing defines and sometimes dictates concepts of humanity and culture, proper social relations, and social behavior. Those who cannot clothe themselves are viewed as socially helpless and dependent on others. Those who refuse to clothe themselves in as little or much as their culture deems appropriate are seen as defiant.

There is a story of a defiant human whose name is Legion, the story of him encountering the one whose name is Son of the Most High God. This is a human who has been stripped of his mind and his community; he stands naked as a jaybird before Jesus, who will also be stripped of his clothing and community before the story's over. But unlike Legion, Jesus' humanity will never be stripped of God. Clothed in the righteousness of God, Jesus prevails over the demonic forces of death that seek to strip life of all meaning. In the making of this disciple, Christ bestows community and clothes, salvation and a call to serve.

Now, I want to ask an interesting question: Where did he get the clothes? Somebody had to give up something. Some one had to share. In order to make disciples we must become involved in the fabric of their lives. We are to be "clothed in righteousness," and from that sheltering grace we draw the connections to clothe the naked and bind the wounds of the wounded. We are charged with re-covering grace in a world that suffers from a nakedness of God.

There are demonic forces that break connections, unravel the work of God's hands. We are called to weave and to reweave the text and texture of the Spirit. The threads of our connections must be spun again and again.

What does the clothing of the community of Jesus look like? If we don't dress for success, what do we wear?

She was the best dressed member of the class of women who gathered for a mission study. We studied the story of the demoniac and pondered the question about his clothes. I gave the class time to create images of what their rags of suffering would look like and to tell stories of what they would wear if they could dress in garments of joy.

She listened carefully and said nothing. When the others brought up pictures to share, she stayed in her seat. After the class was over, she waited until everyone else was gone, and then she asked, "Could I wear my clothes of suffering tomorrow?" I was too intrigued to do anything but agree.

She was missing the next morning when the class started and then she swept, I mean, swept into the room. She was wearing a very fine sheet, toga style. I took my place with the rest, eager to hear her story.

She told it without a trace of self-pity, told it bare-faced, standing there wearing nothing but a bed sheet. She was raised in a foster-care institution, not because she had no parents, but because her mother didn't want her. She remembers being four years old and holding her mother's hand as they climbed the big gray steps and entered the long dark hallway. She remembers crying herself to sleep that night and how the sheets smelled musty and strange.

She remembers a visit when she was nine. Her mother is in the car but won't get out, and she tries to kiss her mother through the window that is half open. She clearly remembers being sent for when she turns fourteen, for now her mother is living with a man who runs a restaurant, and they need a cheap waitress.

She finds a kind man when she turns seventeen and trades in the dirty aprons, the smelly towels, the smeared tablecloths for a plain wedding ring. He's a kind man. They work hard together and do well. She can afford nice things and does.

What she's never been able to figure out until yesterday morning is why she's addicted to sheets. Fine sheets, three hundred thread count, Egyptian cotton, top-of-the-linen-line sheets. She has closets of nothing but sheets. And now she knows what it means.[7] Rags of suffering can't be transformed into garments of joy unless they're washed in the blood of the lamb. They can't get clean until they pass through the waters of baptism with Jesus.

She tells us the story of Jesus, using nothing but images of cloth. She tells it from the swaddling cloth to the linen napkin in the tomb. She finishes and stands for a moment, looking down at what she's wearing.

"She died and I never let it show. Maybe I can explain about these sheets to my pastor. Maybe he'll let me put one on the table when we have communion. Maybe he could preach about forgiveness. Maybe I can feel more at home."

. . .

THEY [MEN AND WOMEN] USED SYMBOLS IN DIFFERENT WAYS. Men, who were dominant, used symbols . . . to renounce their dominance. Reversals and oppositions were at the heart of how symbols worked for men. . . . To women, however . . . symbols of self were in general taken from biological or social experience and expressed not so much reversal or renunciation of worldly advantage as the deepening of ordinary human experience that came when God impinged upon it.[8]

Soul Salsa

Now is the winter of our discontent.
An April ice
can frost any fire in the belly.
Global warming remains science fiction
in a season so rough in its going
that even the tough can't get traction.
we're all slip/sliding away.

'Tis the time when divine worship descends to work ethic questions:
"Parking lot plowed? Furnace turned on?"
We who gather together
pass our prayer time plotting
to burn all of the empty pews
so there's standing room only for Easter.

Wind chill is a factor
of orthodox thought.
The mystery of Trinity
becomes warmly real
in the fellowship hall after church.
Cold-shouldered solitude
is not what we seek in a savior.

What we need is a change in our diet.
Turn grape juice into tequila.
Trade pita for jalapenos.
Santo! Santo! Santo! Hallelujah.

What we have is a lean Lenten map,
marked by sweat, rimmed with salt.
But touch your tongue
to the handwritten legend:
"Here's the heart's desert zone"
and the trace of wild honeycomb.

What we need is the memory of heartburn.
What we need is the salsa of life,
a double-serving of Pentecost heat
for this three-alarm chilly affair.

It's time, and past time to post a church sign:
"We've all gone south of the border."[9]

Pack up Your Troubles in Your Old Kit Bag

I'M A BAG LADY. It's been that way all my life. Purses never suited me; there was never enough room for the "just in cases." Perhaps I knew I'd be singing "On the Road Again" for most of my life. It's easier to accessorize these days since it's entered the middle school market, but in style or out, I pack a backpack. It's also what our grandfathers, vintage WWI, would have called "a kit bag."

One of the motivations of pilgrimage is knowing that someone's waiting a little further down the road. Christ has gone before us. We learn to travel light, looking for the signs of the Spirit, tracking the way of the One who is our truth and our life.

We hope we've kept someone waiting. Our beloved saints hover out of reach but not out of mind. All those who have gone before remain out of sight, just beyond our hearing. We expect to see them at the next turn of the road, but they're further on. We arrive at a crossroads, packing our grief and spices to bury the dead, and discover they are gone. Any hope of reunion is in the One who meets us, not in the tomb, but in any place where love's redeeming work is done.

Knapsack Annie taught me this. She may be the reason I don't carry purses. We caught up with her on a road between New Mexico and Arizona. We were on our annual summer pilgrimage from east to west and back again. My parents had Depression habits of travel; they picked up hitchhikers and often took them home.

She was striding ahead, thumb out, but not begging. She would get where she was going, with or without a ride. My father slowed to a stop and the four of us girls sighed in unison and moved over to make room for her pack bag behind the seat. She was an ugly woman; her face matched her sack. Her road smell made us wrinkle our noses and whisper behind our hands in the back seat. She soon enchanted us with stories of the road, stories of adventure. She understood the lure of the horizon. She described places she'd seen that I still dream of seeing. She seemed a free woman, unafraid to go her way and hold her own, with nothing but a backpack for home.

Of course my mother invited her to stay with us and she did for several weeks. We came to breakfast one morning to find her gone. She left a note, explaining that she had trouble with alcohol. She'd done well but could feel herself slipping. She didn't want us to see her when she fell off the wagon. I think our grandmother had to explain what the wagon was and why people fell off even when they didn't want to.

Years later, after we were grown, a postcard arrived the Sunday after Easter. It was from Knapsack Annie. She'd found herself on a park bench on Easter Sunday, across from a church. She remembered us, straightened her clothes, tried to get in and join the singing. Some usher stopped her cold at the front door. She wanted us to know she'd remembered meeting us, hoped to see us again somewhere down the road.

I still look for her every Easter morning. I know my foot comes off the gas when I see someone on the road, and sometimes I ignore all the travel advice and stop and ask where they're going. Why not imagine church as a company of footloose and fancy-free hitchhikers of galaxies heading for the next horizon, singing as they go? "Pack up your troubles in your old kit bag and smile, smile, smile." That usher, wherever he is, might have trouble catching a ride.

The First Breakfast

So where would he host the first breakfast?

In a sanctuary of saints with the scent of hothouse lilies?
Or a megachurch crowd where wide screen resurrection
is all a matter of timing?
A quaint country church with proud plastic flowers
and Last Supper codes on the wall?

A Sunday brunch for breakfast?
That wasn't his style first time around
And probably won't be his last.

Maybe a diner
if it has ham and eggs served sunnyside up.
Definitely a diner
if coffee comes in a cup with your name.
Clearly a diner
if it has a touch of class in the placemats
and green leaves painted on glass.

It has to be an all night or first light diner
where underfed folk find a reason
to swallow hope
hook, line, and sinker.
Then it's time to tip the cook
and take a stroll down by the riverside,

to check the tides, tinker with boats,
and watch for whale sign
when it's in season.[10]

This was written for the owners, cooks, and waitresses at a diner along the Delaware River in the Garden State. A whale with a poor sense of direction sailed up the river during Holy Week and hung around the river's edge for most of the week till he found his bearings. The festive mood his presence created at the diner became a "sign of Jonah," evidence of resurrection.

Heavenly Hospitality

For as in baptism, God, regenerating us, engrafts us into the society of his church and makes us his own by adoption, so we have said, that he discharges the function of a provident householder in continually supplying to us the food to sustain and preserve us in that life into which he has begotten us by his Word.

—Calvin, "Means of Grace," in *Institutes*

Perhaps it was the shrimp.
It made a first impression
that the chocolate concoction
did nothing to correct.

Is . . .
We inhale bliss between bites.

Is it . . .
We sandwich astonishment softly.

Is it possible . . .
We spear hope hors d'oeuvre.

Is it possible that . . .
We gravitate to the punch line.

Eucharist
is a magnanimous matter,
not a pusillanimous affair?

Is it possible that God
even God
will table every lean and hungry motion
in the end?[11]

—*for Bard and Bert Thompson*

two STORIES AND STRUCTURES
OF FORGIVENESS

W hat does it mean to say, "I believe in the forgiveness of sins"? How does one practice asking for and offering forgiveness outside a sanctuary? We have prayers of confession and assurances of pardon, but too few structures and stories for living the truth in love. Forgiveness is gut-wrenching, mind-bending, and plain awe-full work. Where does the will for putting wrong things right come from?

There are some situations of injury so severe that we must raise the question as to whether forgiveness is possible, and if possible, the right thing to desire. How is justice served when evil goes unpunished? Can we forgive if we never forget?

Forgiveness requires the work of memory as well as the work of mourning; as Paul Ricoeur writes, "an actual memory consists in the presence to the mind of an image—an *icon*—representing an absent thing, namely an event which occurred earlier, that is before we evoke it, declare it, or tell a story about it."[1]

These icons of lost or absent things in the mind cannot be invented, but they can be evoked. We go looking for that which has been lost or left behind by naming it, telling stories about this image/memory. In place of the actual lost object, or a loss of integrity or innocence, we re-create what we're grieving for within our memory where it can be retrieved whenever we reach for it. Nostalgia and despair can make forgiveness impossible, but often when these stories of loss are shared, our private search for consolation can become a communal source of healing. We need, however, to lay hands on the hard edges that have wounded us. We need to get our stuff together. We evoke it. We declare it. We tell a story about it. It is the first sound of forgiveness.

Stained Glass

I HAD BEEN INVITED to design the worship services for a ministers' retreat. I asked for an image or an icon that would describe the general mood and mind of this particular gathering. "Broken" was one answer. "Fragmented" was another. "Angry/hurting" was the third.

The retreat design called for an opening service of preaching and a concluding service of communion. The same room was to be used for work and worship. The physical space was limited, so Laura Tenzel, a liturgical designer, helped me create a hands-on structure of memory and mourning both corporate and personal.

Broken glass. Sharp cuts. Blood stains. Stained glass. These were the images that surfaced as I reviewed the bits and pieces of this service. Many of the pastors and musicians gathering in this retreat spent their lives surrounded by stained glass. There was no stained glass in the space in which we were going to work and worship. What would it mean to create a piece of stained glass from the broken, hurting pieces of this community's life?

Finding the pieces of stained glass from a local artist was the easy part. How would we bring the people and the glass together without causing further damage? How could we help the community to recollect itself? Privacy needed recognition; fingers needed protection. "Gift wrap the pieces" was the answer, so wrap it we did, in fading pages of paperback copies of *The Good News for Modern Man*. Each broken piece, with its own distinction of color and edge, was wrapped in a page of the good news.

The stained glass is to be used as a reverse offering, in response to the preached word. During the first service, the congregation is invited to lay hands on their sense of brokenness, to come forward and receive their sharp-edged piece of memory. The large basket will be left beside the door after the last service for those who might not want to take a piece in front of others.

I give only one instruction: they are to keep their piece of stained glass until the closing communion. They are to unwrap it and read its wrapping. There will be an opportunity to return it during the last service.

We need to breathe memory in and out like oxygen. We need to be heard in order to know we're alive. The first things we need to say may be sounds of lament, but we need to evoke memory, declare it, and tell stories about it. Narratives of gospel and glass start as soon as the glass is unwrapped. The written words on the wrapping are drawn into the stories of mourning. The randomness begins to be interpreted as revelation. This symbol of ecclesiastical stain and shattering permits light to pass through.

Two men, once old friends, now deeply embittered by a rivalry of appointments, meet in a hallway the day after the glass was given. Instead of passing without a word as they have for years, they stop, spontaneously extending to the other the piece of glass they are carrying. Some version of this exchange happens over and over again in the days that follow. The tangible evangelism creates new narratives of forgiveness.

I'm having lunch when the no-nonsense bishop presents himself at my table and announces, "I want you to know that I don't believe in any of this woo-woo stuff." I'm at a loss to respond. What was "woo-woo" stuff? I knew I was in the south, but I thought I understood the dialect. "Explain this," he demands and slaps his piece of glass and its wrapping down on the table. I unwrap it and look at the page. He's underlined one passage. I recognize it. It's his text for the closing service that was printed in the bulletin two weeks earlier. "So," he says. "Explain how I picked that out of all the rest." I grin and quote from the gospel of John. "You did not choose me but I chose you."

The final structure of this iconic glass cannot be completed within the time frame of the conference. Some forms of forgiveness require a long time to gestate; sacramental things grow slowly into their proper shape. The finishing of this work of stained glass and forgiveness comes a year later. I ask a minister of the conference who is a gifted visual artist if he will take responsibility for the glass that would be collected as people came for communion.

He's silent for a long time. I think he's going to refuse, and then he begins to talk about the sudden death of his brother, who was a stained glass artist. He asks for the pieces. A year later, a stained glass image of a cross has emerged from the fragments of glass. I receive a picture of this icon with a note that tells me what he couldn't say before, that his brother died from AIDS. Forgiveness assembles the broken shards of memory and mourning. Healing shines through the stain.

> The time has come to listen to an other, a silent but non-mute voice, and to look at a shining, blinding light—that of forgiveness. I am saying a non-mute voice since it has its appropriate discourse, namely that of the *hymn*, the discourse of praise and celebration. And what does it say? Merely that *there is* forgiveness.[2]

The Wedding Garment

DOES GOD ALWAYS FORGIVE? There's a terrifying story about what seems to be an unforgivable social sin in the twenty-second chapter of the gospel of Matthew. Picture the setting. You've just crashed a wedding reception; not crashed exactly, you're there because of a hearsay invitation from a friend of a friend of the third groomsman. You check out the name cards and pick out a head table that just says "Reserved." The music's great, the bar's open, and there's more than enough food to go around. You check out who sits where, who's taking cuts, who's dancing with the bride. You're a little underdressed, but you intend to make a great impression as soon as you can find the host. You've got your best interests at heart. You know how to work it. Head of the class, head of the line; start at the bottom, head of the firm in no time. You've just got to catch your host's eye.

Not much forgiveness in this story. Not only is the underdressed guest publicly shamed in front of everyone, he gets tossed by a well-armed bouncer and dumped into the trash pits of hell. It's a dangerous story to leave lying around. It needs to be handled carefully. A good preacher can usually open the cage of this snarling story and not get bitten. A gifted teacher can draw out the tension: feast on the good news that the one who creates, redeems, and sanctifies the cosmos is your host. You'd better know who invited you and come prepared to celebrate, because there's no free lunch in this story, just the terrifying beauty, justice, and love of the banquet house of God.

So what about forgiveness? Does forgiveness redeem shame as well as guilt? A child once explained the difference between shame and guilt. "Guilt is what you can talk about. Shame is what you can't." Is there a language we can learn for what we can't say? Does the work of memory and mourning offer us release from the toxic waste dumps of shame?

I know a way out of hell. It's the story of a wedding garment, a robe to wear at Christ's table. A class of sixth graders attending a conference on music and worship made a chasuble, a vestment worn when presiding at the sacrament of the table. Each child picked an image to paint: flowers, bread, a crown, fish, a cup, a rainbow, and one Purple Heart (makes you wonder what that kid knew about discipleship).

They were making the chasuble for me to wear, but because I was involved somewhere else in the conference, I never got to meet the children. Every day I went by to see it after my workshop, and there were more and more colorful images added to the robe.

When I came in on the third day, I spotted an unwelcome addition. It was a messy scrawl, a purple, black, and blue cross stuck in at an awkward angle, hanging on the edges of the garment like a bruise. I remember thinking "Why didn't Laura have that kid hand out pencils rather than draw?" I decided to make sure this is on the backside when I put it on.

The service was arranged so that I would preach, and when the offering of the elements was carried to the table, a child of the class would bring the robe forward and help me dress for the Christ's table. So I preach, and turn and wait; the people are singing. The gift bearer is on his way, but it takes him a long time to reach to me.

I know immediately who drew the cross. I'm speechless with shame. I'm not sure I dare come near the table. His face is shining like a star as he slowly walks toward me with the fierce concentration that cerebral palsy requires. I know I've been judged. I'm unfit to preside at the table. Every arrogant notion that God can only be served by beauty and that only the able-bodied belong to the body of Christ got stripped away. I'm stark naked and ashamed. I get on my knees while the child dresses me. He has to help me stand.

This is a story that still makes me tremble. We are called to the table by the One who is our judge as well as our redeemer. Some truth begins to dawn—such as that we can't dress ourselves. We must be covered by the forgiveness of Christ when we come to the table.

Strawberry Fields Forever

Q: When is a house not a home?

A: When it belongs to God.

After twenty-five years of itinerant ministry, I found myself weary of structures called parsonages. To nail or not to nail up a picture? Who pays to have the third-story windows washed? What about the two-inch scratch on the pressed wood coffee table, or a trustee who monitors how long the light in the basement is on?

I began to pay more attention to the horror stories of retired pastors who have to live in chicken houses or with their children. We needed to find our own piece of ground, build a roof and four walls that we can paint purple if it suits our fancy.

Be careful what you pray for. At the end of a vacation of nonstop labor on my family's farm, Bill and I are the puzzled possessors of a smokehouse. It was built just after the War. (In West Virginia, that's the War between the States.) It's a gift, we're told. I think of it more as a burden, but since we own nothing else that might qualify as a retirement home, we decide to take it seriously.

A smokehouse isn't part of a regular real estate market. One might not know what it is or at least what it used to be. It's a primitive structure, a basic link in the food chain, a place and process for preparing animals for human consumption. Here is where the pioneer family who farmed this land slaughtered, hung, gutted, and smoked the deer, the squirrels, the coons, the pigs, the calves, the lambs.

The end result of a smokehouse is smoked meat, the basic staple for survival in premodern farm life. Its original function is still on display, since two meat hooks hang down from the ceiling just to the right of the doorway. You can lose an eye if you're not careful. The hooks have been left because of my family's weird sense of humor and history.

I start my inventory of the state of my new real estate that's built of old wood with old stains, old sins, and the odd odors of blood, smoke, and grease. It's enough to make a vegetarian out of me if I think about it for very long. I decide to leave the hooks hanging. It's a very visible call to prayer, a reminder that we are to be altered by what we eat. *Lamb of God that taketh away the sins of the world, have mercy on us.* I begin to think that fire would be a better solution to restructuring. My penance for having those thoughts is to arrange for fire insurance; that will guarantee that only an act of God will take this structure down.

Two of the walls that form the back porch are home to wild honey bees. If we had money, we'd spray and replace the old wood with top-of-the-line tongue-and-groove board. Since we don't, we wait until early evening and use the country form of climate control: tar paper. The bee stragglers who arrive after dark find their entrance has been sealed with crisp black paper marked with parallel white lines. It's a guide for those who can't nail in a straight line.

What else have I inherited, besides the meat hooks and the wild bees? A kitchen with every odd end including a kitchen sink and a large hole in the corner ceiling for the six-foot black snake that keeps uninvited guests on edge. Seven stair steps to the upper floor currently serve as a bookcase for the *World Encyclopedia*, volumes 7–11. A postmodern metal cupboard, painted by one of my son's tribe of Lost Boys. They spent a summer here making music that drew neighbors and scared away the mice.

I find a scrapbook with an antique Spanish map on its cover on the stairs between volumes 8 and 9. I sit down to look at it. Asia is circled in red with a magic marker. Tibet, India, and Persia are the only legible names. Drawn at the edge of the Oceana Orientale is a sea monster with human eyes. The scrapbook belongs to the last family who lived here, boat refugees from Cambodia. It's passing strange to find it on the day that Pol Pot, former leader, dictator, monster of the Khmer Republic, dies at home, apparently at peace.

The first page of this "Magic Magnetic Photos" album (made in Japan) holds a handwritten note, dated September 14, 1979. "For our new friends, the Mwong family, from Frank Turnbull's brother Bill and wife Mary who live at 76 Edgerton Rd. in Akron Ohio." On the first page is part of a news clipping:

Refugee family finds peace with West Virginia family.

Frank and Ellen Turnbull planned a quiet life on their farm in Wirt County when the last of their eight children started to college this fall. That was before they started the chain of events that brought a Cambodian refugee family to share their home high in the hills of West Virginia. Now, for the past month, Lem Loang, his wife, Sua Chit and their four children are living with the retired Presbyterian minister and wife on their farm on the Sonoma-Blue Goose Road which borders Roane County. It all began, according to Rev. Turnbull, with letters from his brother, Robert, who is a missionary in Thailand. These letters told of the tragic situation for the many Cambodian families arriving in the camps in Thailand. "We screwed up our courage and wrote to the Task Force for Resettlement of Refugees at our church headquarters in New York, said Rev. Turnbull. The Presbyterian Church in Spencer agreed to also sponsor the family and to back up the Turnbulls in their adoption of the refugee family.

The homeless family arrived with nothing but the clothes on their back. They knew no English and no one could speak their Khmer language. But they brought with them gentleness, a willingness to help, and an eagerness to learn that immediately won the hearts of the Turnbulls and all who meet them.

"Right from the moment they arrived, Sua Chit and her fifteen-year-old daughter, Kim Nahm, have stepped right in and helped me with the work," said Ellen Turnbull. "We have to communicate with love and with sign language, but they catch on very quickly," she added. "The father, Lem, is literate in his native tongue," explained Rev. Turnbull. "He studied in a monastery to be a monk before . . ."

The clipping ends here. Beside it is a Christmas card, depicting the darker side of the nativity: the flight into Egypt. There another handwritten note in the corner of the card, just above the figure of a weary Joseph who is leading a dejected looking donkey: "Lem, there is so much beauty in your love. I know when you learn of this, you will rejoice." Above the figure of Mary who's holding on to her child for dear life, is written "This card of Mary and Joseph and the baby Jesus so reminded me of you and yours, Sua Chit."

What is this doing here? It's part of the history, the inheritance, the story of this smoky structure. It is also an example of the difficulties with forgiveness. What is the difference between amnesty and amnesia?[3]

Once upon a time in a country called Cambodia . . . and so the unspeakable history begins. It helps us resist amnesia by listing what is known to be fact. On October 8, 1968, forty thousand North Vietnamese troops invade Cambodia with Prince Sihanouk's permission. On April 30, 1969, U.S. and South Vietnamese troops invade Cambodia. Large antiwar protests break out in the United States and Europe. The U.S. troops are withdrawn by June 29. On October 9, 1969, there is a formal proclamation of the Khmer Republic.

For several years, headlines in Cambodia don't register on the national news of the average U.S. citizen. Then, in 1973, twice as many U.S. bombs are dropped on Cambodia as were dropped on Japan in World War II. By August, Congress forces the president and the military to end U.S. bombing.

By 1975, Khmer Rouge communist forces control Phnom Penh and two-thirds of the country. A new leader, Pol Pot, is now head of Kampuchea, the new name of the republic. He will personally oversee the execution of hundreds of thousands of the "exploiting" classes: army officers, civil servants, teachers, monks, and nuns. Hundreds of thousands of Cambodians flee the country as refugees in the next four years.

There are four thousand public confessions in 1976, followed by executions. Nearly two million people are either massacred or worked to death in labor camps. The Khmer Rouge communists execute nearly every member of the educated classes in Cambodia between 1975 and 1979.[4]

The family that takes shelter in the smokehouse on Spring Creek walks four hundred miles to escape. They lose family members in the jungle, in the refugee camps, and at the borders of the United States.

The basic kindness of our Spring Creek neighbors, the Turnbulls, opens the door to Almost Heaven. Immigration regulations require that the head of the house be employed. They need work. Our folks just happen to have an abandoned smokehouse and a farm. I often wondered what kind of karmic chaos we caused, however, by putting Cambodian Buddhists in a renovated slaughterhouse.

They start to earn their keep with sheep that had been abandoned when my oldest sister's husband went MIA after the war in Vietnam was over. The Mwongs lack the skill, not the will to learn, but sheep can be downright self-destructive without a good shepherd. They don't know that sheep seek shade during the day. When they huddle in the barn the family would drive them outside to graze. It made the sheep crazy. It probably made the Buddhists crazy, raising lambs for slaughter.

My grandmother would have understood. She hated the smell of the smokehouse and limited its use during her farming days. She did what a farmer's wife was supposed to do—raise animals for slaughter—but she didn't want blood shed on her land, her ground. She loved the lambs best, and named her favorites, Thunder and Lighting. Her grown children remember how the lambs cried and she cried when they had to be sold to pay a doctor's bill.

There's a child's drawing of a heart (perhaps it's a heart; it's colored bright red) on the third page. Cambodian hearts in Appalachia: homesick, heart-shy Buddhists in Almost Heaven. The warm-hearted kindness of strangers led them to the Promised Land. But the loneliness must have bitten bone deep like the wind. I study the child's heart in the scrapbook again. Perhaps it's a strawberry. It turned out to be the answer to prayer. From the Killing Fields to Strawberry Fields Forever.

They were good at growing strawberries. From this window in the smokehouse you can see where their fields once stretched, for miles, it seemed.

Of course, the view is a little crooked since the two rooms added to the smokehouse were built by a church committee. The rooms were well built, with the best of intentions, but lacked a firm foundation, so they began to sag as soon as gravity and moisture got to them.

The family finds shelter in this structure for four years until they get their bearings. They locate other family members in North Carolina, get jobs in the factories, and, like other rural farmers, migrate to a big city. They send a photo of their firstborn in a Christmas card. It's pasted beside the drawing of the strawberry heart.

I study these bookends of Christmas cards and wonder about their message of forgiveness "When you learn of this . . ." is written on the first card, but what is the lesson? What part of the Christmas story didn't they know? The flight for life? The massacre of innocents? The horror of holocaust? The kindness of strangers? The forgiveness of God?

Once I saw their father, Lem, use sign language to tell what happened to some of those left behind. One only has to read the ancient curse of the psalmist to understand what he couldn't bear to say, only try to show: "Happy shall they be who take your little ones and smash them against the rock!"

> Amnesty is both a political and juridical act the finality of which is to cure the wounds of the social body. This discretionary act raises the disquieting question of the boundary between amnesty and amnesia. This boundary would be preserved if, on the one hand, the reason for not forgetting were kept in mind . . . and, on the other hand the rationale proper to amnesty were properly acknowledged: the good health of the common City.[5]

What did forgiveness come to mean to these gentle Buddhists? Perhaps only what they already believed, that hospitality matters, no matter what the religion. Is forgiveness possible? Or just amnesia? The ruling party's recent offer of complete amnesty to members of the Khmer Rouge comes without a requirement of any kind of public accountability. Will this cure the wounds of the social body? God only knows. But if we believe in the whole Christmas story it means we're supposed to offer room, whether it is an inn or a smokehouse, for the stranger, the alien, the homeless, even our enemy. We do this because we've been told. "Inasmuch," he said.

We prepare to shelter any child, even the children of our enemies in whatever structure of our life can withstand the terrors of history. We do this because we believe that God so loved . . . The unknown scrapbook writer gets it right: "There is so much beauty in your love."

Dancing the Hula in Heaven

IT'S SUNDAY AFTERNOON, and I'm still in the office. Being suddenly elevated or, more precisely, "elevatored" into the bureaucracy of an academic institution disorients one's sense of Sabbath. The phone rings and brings the news that the wife of a colleague is in intensive care following exploratory surgery. The verdict wasn't good going in and now it's reached the bottom line. Her cancer is too extensive; surgery is out of the question. She is living on borrowed time. I call the dean, who's away at a conference, and relay the plans for pastoral care that I'm putting into place. The chaplain's on the way, flowers have been ordered, a prayer request has been given to the chapel committee, the news reported to other faculty colleagues.

"Forget the chaplain," he says. "You're the academic dean. You need to go." I find myself gripping a paperweight like a lifeline or a grenade. I don't say a word, but he hears the argument loud and clear. "If you want to be a dean," he says, "you've got to be dean of all, not just some."

I take a deep breath, and bite my tongue. I could make a good case that my presence might be adding insult to injury. I should remind our new dean this assignment might put us all in harm's way. I'm being asked to offer pastoral care to an honest-to-God enemy.

Months before the controversial conference called "Re-Imagining" took place, a war over the biblical Wisdom tradition and women doing theology had been declared in our seminary chapel. I've shed sweat, tears, and blood, spent months of my life gathering hard evidence to prove that what this colleague has written about a service of holy communion is factually wrong and, frankly, wrongheaded. A few of us have been compelled to answer accusations that we are pagans, communists, heretics, Femi-Nazis, promiscuous, and perverse. We've been called everything but children of God.

What I should say is "Stuff it. Not on my life or peace of mind." What I hear myself saying is "Yes." God knows why. Peace of mind is in short supply, although I'm still in one piece.

I've survived the threat of a lawsuit on charges of slander, letters to Drew's Board of Trustees, and a public hearing before six hundred members of my conference about sacramental violation and Reimagining God. My credentials as a Christian, as a feminist, and as a seminary teacher have been challenged, and I'm not even the primary target.

When it's clear I'm going to need a lawyer, I locate one who comes highly recommended. I send him over fifty pounds of documents, including a Book of Discipline of our church. He wants to read everything before he decides to take me as a client. When he finally calls, he tells me that he has one question to ask before he reaches his final decision. I clear my throat and say, "Yes?" His tone is very solemn. "Will representing you, as your attorney, in any way endanger my immortal soul?" I stare at the receiver. That's the question? "How, in God's name, am I supposed to know?" "Good," he says. Now I can almost hear him grin. "An honest client. I'll take your case."

A church trial involving the first United Methodist woman elected bishop in the Northeast is being called. A clergy member has filed a grievance against her based on an article my colleague has written. A leading clergywoman has preached a sermon on God's Wisdom, Sophia, in our chapel. The communion service I've led is cited as an example of goddess worship, even though the critic walked out of the chapel before the invitation to the table was even given. In a strange exercise of sophistry, the bishop, not the preacher or the presider, is accused of failure to uphold her office by not disciplining her clergy with a charge of heresy.

In the end—and it takes nearly a year to reach it—the church body appointed to review the charges find the accusations unfounded, and the account of the service unsupported by other witnesses. They dismiss the grievance against the bishop. The discredited accusations of sacramental violation and liturgical duplicity, however, continue to circulate. I receive tenure, when it's all said and done, and then as evidence that God has a weird sense of humor, I end up in the office of academic dean.

So here I am, new to the office, and I've just received a mission impossible. The dean signs off. I put the phone down, but I'm still gripping the receiver. I'm not alone in this storm. My husband and son were caught in this whirlwind. I've been obsessed with protecting my institution and have failed to notice that our son has been left unarmed. He read a letter from a lawyer threatening to sue the university over my actions and despaired about ever finding a home. He thinks I'll lose my teaching position. He fears having to move again, start over. He's found the itinerant ministry to be hard stony ground. We've failed to keep his soul well watered and his body rooted.

He's thinks he's got nothing to lose, so he tries jumping into the chasm. He takes a bottle of five hundred Valium from the local drugstore where he works, signs his name so they'll know who's to blame. He takes thirty-five before he passes out. It is grace, sheer grace, and perhaps a guardian angel that catches him as he falls. But even guardian angels can't protect you from the long arm of the law. He's arrested after surviving his fall.

I force myself to unlock my fingers from the phone and my mind from this memory. I have to make a pastoral visit to the wife of my enemy. Think. What do I know about her? I finger-comb my memory. We faculty gather along work-related lines these days; it's been years since we and our next of kin were all in the same room together. I recall that she was described as artistic and a free spirit. She led the liturgical dance group in the early '70s and after returning from a trip to Hawaii she offered to teach the seminary's upright faculty how to do the hula.

I decide that my only option is to follow Wesley's Rules: first, do no harm, and second, do all the good you can. I'll bring her something beautiful, link it to a prayer, and keep my visit very brief.

I find a gift shop near the hospital and browse the shelves, looking for something that might serve as a means of grace. On the bottom shelf I find what I need, a woman's figure outlined in a copper metal votive candle. Her hands are lifted as if in prayer. She is the posture of *orans*, the ancient gesture of worship inherited from the

Jews and imprinted on saints and martyrs painted on catacomb walls. Her figure is generous, her hips ample. I can imagine her moving in step with the Lord of the Dance, doing a holy hula, backlit with the flame of prayer. I can have it wrapped and get to hospital a half hour before visiting hours are over. I smile as I watch the saleswoman do her work of gilding the lily. As she ties the bow, she says, "I'm so glad you found our goddess votive. She's one of my favorites."

Goddess. Goddess? "Does it say goddess any where on the votive?" I can hear the shock in my voice. "I don't know," she says. "Do you want me to unwrap it and see? I feel my face freezing up. I've just bought a goddess votive as a gift to a dying woman whose husband has accused me of corrupting a service of Holy Communion with goddess worship. (As Nelle Morton says, "If you ever doubt that "God" is a male word, try saying "Goddess" out loud and see what comes out of the woodwork.")

"Is there," I carefully ask, "anything else connected with a goddess in this store? Anything at all?" "No, I don't think so," she replies. "You found the only one we have."

I shove the gift into the top of my backpack. I've got twenty minutes left and am minus a gift. I race for the hospital entrance. I can only hope he's not there and that she won't have a clue as to who I am.

I'm wrong on both counts. I reach her curtained-off space in the ICU, and just as I see him sitting on the far side, I hear her say, "Why, Heather, it's so good to see you."

Grace is grace because we don't earn it. It's mystery, pure and anything but simple. I go to offer some stiff-necked pastoral care to someone I don't want to know and she calls me by name. She's dying yet she transforms a pallid ICU unit into a place of color and laughter and art with nothing but imagination and memory. She talks about artists she loves, the music she remembers, and the beauty of California. Her one free hand conducts her conversation like a choir. I ask her about her trip to Hawaii and the dancing lesson. He sits just beyond my sight, silent, almost a shadow on the wall.

An orderly enters to check the flow of the fluids that are prolonging her life and keeping pain at bay. She's on morphine but is clear-eyed about being on borrowed time. I shift my chair, preparing for the closing prayer, and my bag tips over, spilling the gift on the floor.

"Oh," she says, pleased like a child. "Oh, is that a gift for me?" I start to babble, trying to stick the box back in my bag. "It's just a small token; better opened at home; it's a candle, but, of course, I should have remembered the oxygen, no flames allowed; it's nothing, really, just something that reminded me of women and prayer and the hula, of course . . ." I'm appalled. I'm babbling.

He rises and stretches out his hand for the gift. She wants to see it. I reluctantly put a weapon of my own demise in his hand. No one will believe my version of this story. I watch with dread as the wrappings come off. "Please," I'm thinking. "Please, no labels." I close my eyes as he lifts it for inspection. The copper outline of She Who Is emerges serene and uncluttered, hands lifted as if in dance or prayer. He holds it out for her to see. She smiles, "Oh, so lovely. I'll put it where I can see it when I get home."

Home? Does she know what her chances are? She smiles. She knows what she means. "May I pray with you before I go?" I ask. "Please." She offers her hand. I stand, take her hand, and move to lightly touch her knee. I am caught by surprise when my right hand is caught in a grip that's tight, and a little too strong. He's holding my hand.

We both know what it should mean, and what it doesn't. It's where I'd drawn the line. This is the right hand of fellowship. It's the way we've welcomed newcomers into our household of Christ for generations. I don't shake hands with my enemy.

I've had to work in the same room, eat at the same table, attend the same meetings with him, but I won't shake his hand. I joined my religious tribe with this gesture; it's a sign of loyalty to loyalty. Even in front of a dean who's trying to fix this festering wound before it spreads, I refuse to take his hand. I try to forgive. Christ knows, I've always been terrified of those three little words in the Lord's Prayer: *as we forgive.* But I can't shake his hand. There is no reconciliation until things are set right.

She's holding my hand so lightly her fingers feel like silk. He's got a grip on my other one; it feels like we're getting ready to arm wrestle. Is this a dare, a threat, a request, a plea? I can't read what he means, but I suddenly know someone's drawn a line in my sand. If I can't do this, if I can't turn loose of memory and ask for God's forgetfulness, I won't be able to lead a congregation in prayer again. "As we forgive . . ."

I know what has to be done. I gather my wits, shift my fingers, and accept his hand. Perhaps only holy forgetfulness makes human forgiveness possible. We join hands, he and I, the right hand of fellowship. We turn toward the one who's been a means of grace. In less than two weeks she'll be gone. I'm asked by the dean not to attend her funeral. I never know why or who doesn't want me. But for now, hand in hand, together we lift her up in prayer.

Through the Eye of a Needle

Pull up your chair to the edge of a chasm, and I will tell you a story.

—attributed to Yeats

THINGS, ONCE PERCEIVED, become an intangible presence within us. They move in, so to speak, take up residence in the rooms of our imagination and memory. This may lead us to hoard our objects of desire until they dispossess our relationships with each other and with God. Treasures can trash our souls. Jesus warns us about the addictiveness of stuff. "For where your treasure is, there your heart will be also" (Matt. 6:21). Here is where an ironic narrative can work as a scalpel cutting away our addiction, self-pity, nostalgia, and self-interest.

A very tangible reminder of the danger that comes from my desire to collect things lies ten feet away from my desk. It's a basket of syringes, with Halloween bright orange caps that almost glow in the dark. I've learned to love needles, at least in a general sense of the word love. They, plus the bottles of insulin, are the tools that keep my partner, my husband, my very smart man, Bill, alive. They are a pain; they are problem solvers. Once they were the cause of a wrong impression and a right conclusion.

I'm in my office, Monday morning, a little worse for wear. Late Saturday night I was handed a million dollar grant to pull into shape, and it's due today at four o'clock. I've been working nonstop, and it's

completely slipped my mind that I have a new administrative assistant due to arrive any minute. Bill has stopped by with food, coffee,
pep talks over the weekend to keep me from pulling out my hair. My
desk is covered with papers, coffee cups, more papers, reports, forms,
reference books, grant guidelines, and on the corner that's not covered is my father's straight edged razor and my husband's used dia-
betic syringe.

Alma, my new assistant, walks in to find me red-eyed, very wired,
and not answering my phone. I look up from my purgatory of margins and budget lines, wave, and tell her that we'll talk later. I don't
note that her eyes have gotten very wide. She checks out the razor,
the used needle, and quietly backs out of the room, closing the door.
She's a street smart mover and shaker from Brooklyn. She knows
what needles mean. I'm addicted. Theological education must be a
tougher neighborhood than she expected. I keep a straight-edged
razor within reach.

She decides she's going to be my first line of defense. She guards
my door all day long, protecting me until I wind down from whatever
I've been using. It's months before she tells me this story. It's been
widened over time to include our daily encounters that put the razor
and a syringe in their proper places. We both know now I am addicted, to work and to collecting strange stuff. It remains one of my
favorite cautionary tales about the dangers of bureaucracy, objects of
desire, and the rare gift of loyalty to loyalty.

Kindness of Strangers

IN THE FALL OF 2001 I'm willingly released from being a dean to spend a semester teaching in a faculty exchange program with Ewha Woman's University in Korea. What follows are messages from my e-mail correspondence with Bill, my husband, during the days immediately before and after September 11, 2001.

September 1

Dear William Wesley:

This is the first e-mail of what promises to be a constant stream of electronic impulses from the mountaintop mission house in Seoul to Drew Forest. Thanks to you and Younglae, I have at least one twenty-first century mode of communication. I'm not counting the old radio I found in the attic yesterday. I don't think it works.

It's very early in the morning and I'm watching the city's horizon switch from natural light to the marketplace reds, greens, bright whites, and gold. It keeps me from losing patience as I try to get on the Internet. I'm going to have to get a cell phone. Only the old grandmothers who sit on the street corners and do their chores while keeping a neighborhood watch seem to be cell-less. I watched five thousand young women pour out of chapel at Ewha and they were all talking to five thousand other young women, God knows where. Having a cell phone is like carrying your own village in your pocket.

The mission house is very noisy for a nearly empty structure. It's gotten louder since you left last week. I check each of the seven bedrooms before I go to sleep and say goodnight to the ghosts of the great mission projects of Methodism. I'm haunted by the stories of Thanksgiving gatherings, Bible studies in the dining room, and children's games in the enclosed garden. There's a smell of abandonment that I can't disburse with scented candles. The unkempt beds and musty covers, the rusty water from the faucets, the puzzles and books are all signs of abandonment. It's driving me crazy, wanting to fix what's broken. I need to remember what you quoted about Paul Riceour. There's something unrepairable about human life.

It's more than entropy; it's unrepairableness. I can forgive entropy, or at least understand it. I don't understand this broken vision, this secret garden and mission house going to rot in a city where space is more precious than blood.

September 4

I've just been bumped off again. I hope you're more forgiving than this server. It's harder every morning to answer your questions. "Why do you have to go to South Korea? Why you? Why now?" How can I explain that this impossible mission had my name in its file? What rational sense would I make when I say that I followed a spoon home, or that I got infected from my father's razor? Setting up a faculty exchange program with the largest women's university in the world satisfies nearly everyone else as a reason. I wonder if you'll ever forgive this much absence? Isn't education salvation? Your painful reproach remains. "Why you? Why now?" I can't answer.
By the way, you forgot your hat.

September 6

Notes on my absent husband's hat:
Or should that be "present husband from whom I'm absent"?
Or is it not a matter of present or absent
but a question of being tardy?
Tardy, then.
I'm certainly guilty of
being behind
one step
one beat
of the heart's proper punctuality.

This hat is my witness:
A lousy sense of timing
can bend the brim of the future
and set the straw on fire.

Sometimes it sits on a shelf,
pensive as its audience.
Sometimes it sits on my head,
adjusting to the strange terrain.
Sometimes its estranged shape presses down
on the question: "Here's your hat.
What's your hurry?"

Perhaps I can learn to make the hat happy.
Practice till I'm perfectly on time
in the right place. With the right space
between my ears. Between my legs.
Within memory. Without guile.

No wonder the matchless Paul insisted
that hair-brained women of highbrow men
should never address the deity hatless.
Proper head covering is more than a matter of style.[6]

September 9

I unpacked Dad's straight-edged razor and put it beside the laptop, Bill. I'm either going to use it on the cables or my wrists. Lucent Technology is stalled in its tracks . . . make that circuits, not tracks. No matter what I've tried today, I can't make the world turn to the west. I may have to stand on the mountain and try shouting "Yahoo" in your direction.

I'm getting fond of the iconic dog on my screen. He comes out of his doghouse whenever I need company and wags his tail waiting for me to write something right. It's the only occasion I feel good about being barked at when I do something wrong.

I've finally written down what I remember whenever I think about Korea. Or this is what I've actively constructed from my memory and imagination. You know the razor story is one of the few relics of my father as a soldier.

You thought it was funny that it was one of the first things I carried into my office. I simply empowered the story by linking it with the object itself. This is the instrumental side of my intuitive life of things. Students, staff, colleagues saw the straight-edged razor on my desk and raised their eyebrows. Sometimes they asked. Sometimes they just looked. A razor's a very unforgiving thing for an academic dean to display. If they'd listen to the story, they'd know it isn't about forgiveness, but about not giving in.

Fifty-one years is a long time to stand guard against chaos and despair, though. I don't think I have it in me. I'm glad I packed it in my trunk, though I was surprised no one objected coming through customs. I'm going to use it when I'm asked to preach, so I thought I'd give the translator a head start on the text:

What does it take to win a war? Five months? Five years? Fifty years? In 1950, a war began here, in the Land of Morning Calm. My father landed with his unit in Inchon. He and hundreds of other Appalachian men had volunteered to serve their country a second time. He was a combat engineer; his job was to build bridges and roads, to support the front lines by getting them where they needed to go in order to win. But the war was going badly, and the troops were in retreat, and his job with the other corps of engineers was to serve as a buffer. He and his outfit were to stand between the retreating officers and their equipment and the advancing enemy.

Standing in between requires an endurance difficult to describe. Like many who survived this standing between, and the long-awaited truce that didn't end the war, just postponed the fighting, he had little to say. Except for a story about a razor.

My father's father taught him to shave with a straight-edged razor. "A man," he told him, "a man shaves every day. Rich or poor. Sick or well. Shaving keeps the world in order, inside you and out. Every day."

So my father shaved. Through the end of a Great Depression. Through the battles of WWII. Through the War between the North and the South of the Land of Morning Calm. One morning, well before dawn, he was positioned with his unit on the hillside south of Seoul. They were in retreat, trying to keep the officers and the tanks from falling into enemy hands. He'd just finished his daily discipline, had just crawled down the hillside to a stream to find water and shave, and then crawled back to his foxhole before the Chinese guns began firing.

The guns began booming and over the sound of the explosions he heard his lieutenant shouting his name. He was surprised, knew something was wrong because the lieutenant and the other officers were supposed to be on the far side of the hill, heading south. But here was this officer who'd crawled back over the hill shouting for him. When he saw my father wave, he shouted a question, "Murray, did you shave today?" My father recalls, "I didn't answer right off. I couldn't make sense of the question. He had to ask me again." "Murray, did you *&%# shave today?" "Yes!" my father shouted. "Why?" "By God," the officer shouted back. "By God, we just might win this!"

Unwearied patience. Unbroken discipline. If that's what it takes to win a war, what does it take to make peace? Basic training in strategies of love. Heart-fueled works of justice and mercy. Training in the armaments of light and truth. Practice in resisting the temptation of bitterness, hatred, despair. More prayer, more work at forgiving enemies who sometimes turn into friends of Christ. Never forget that others may depend on small acts of faithfulness. And the reason we can hold our ground, even in the most desperate of times, is that we do not have to win this war. This war has already been won.

Let me know what you think of what I wrote, Bill. I spent the rest of this morning shopping for the faculty picnic. I'm inviting my new colleagues at Ewha to join me in the secret garden and have lunch. I'm hosting this for the future, but also for the ghosts.

September 11, 2001*

The e-mail's down, the phones are down. All flights have been cancelled. I don't know where or how you are or what's happened to Daniel or Brucie and Barry. I'm writing these messages to send whenever the world rights itself again. I'm acting as if all will be well if I simply keep on keeping on. The radio's on 24-7. It works, thank you, Jesus. The flat-tone announcer of the military news is a lifesaver. It keeps the anguish at bay.

I keep telling myself that you never go to New York on Mondays. I pray Brucie left her apartment and went to Pennsylvania. I'm glad Daniel is in Chicago, but I worry about all our students who live in New York. I walked down to get groceries and water, and everyone stared, but no one spoke. I feel like a ghost.

September 13

Still no word from you, but I was able to read a general e-mail from Drew today while at Ewha. You must be well; it said that the faculty and students are safe. What a gift, what a relief. I can start breathing again. But the others, oh, the others.

I need to take a cab across the river to be fingerprinted. All Americans have been ordered to report their whereabouts and be fingerprinted. They've stationed young men with submachine guns in front of all the American businesses, even McDonald's. Rev Cho of the Chung Dong Methodist Church came to invite me to attend a memorial service at his church tomorrow for the victims of the . . . what do we call what just happened? I'm not sure if I'm to assist in the service, or just be there, but he said that he would introduce me to the new U.S. ambassador, who's just arrived. Everyone is wondering if the president will continue to support the peacemaking work between the North and South.

I think this war, this "unholy" war, was declared a long time ago. Why do we think strapping on our guns and walking out into the world's streets will end this drama? An old woman at the service promises to pray for me. I'm startled. "No, not for you," she corrects herself. "For America. Now you will have to learn what we know. What it means to

*Technically September 12, South Korea time

be at war all your life." One of the Korean veterans of Vietnam said simply, "This will be like fighting the Viet Cong on a global level."

I'm working on a poem that is too hard to handle, but I'm letting it take its time. One of the international students sang "Amazing Grace" for me in my class. It's been as if I'm in free fall. I'm sure everyone will have a story about where they were when it happened. I think we can survive anything if we can talk about it, but this is therapeutic autobiography on a global level.

I hope I hear from you before the day's over. Other people have begun to get through on the landline phones, but my cell phone cuts off every time I call. I wouldn't have known what was happening there without it. Younglae made arrangements for it on September 9, may he be happy forever! It rang about midnight two days later; woke me up and I couldn't figure out how to answer it for several minutes. When I did get it on, nothing made sense. It was some woman who was very upset. She kept switching between Korean and English and the words like "war" and "trade center" made no sense. She offered to come over, but I was so confused with the message that I thanked her and hung up.

I remember sitting there, staring at it, and wondering if disassociation was one of the signs of severe culture shock. Surely someone I know would tell me if the world was ending? By the time I call you fifteen times and then everyone whose number I have it's almost one o'clock in the morning. I get my Korean/English dictionary and look up the word "war." I feel like an utter fool, but I'm a desperate one. I walk outside the gates and knock at the first house that has a light on. A man comes to the door, and I try to say something, God knows what, about a war. He simply opens the door and invites me in. His wife is watching TV in the living room. I get a glimpse of the first plane, the tower, the second plane, then the smoke, then the fall. They offer tea. I watch the images again, searching for Brucie's apartment. I see it in the first screen, and then it disappears when the tower goes down. I get up, thank them, and go back to the mission house. I sit up all night, trying the cell phone, the e-mail, the prayer channel.

September 14

No news is not good news. I find myself reciting a verse that I wrote years ago in a poem called "The Waiting." What did Sarah do during the seven days it took Abraham to discover that God didn't want fathers to sacrifice their sons?

The morning spreads like spilt wine,
And soaks the thirsty sand of my eyes.
Three dawns met in patience.
With the fourth rises fear.
I have worn a hole in the door flap
 Like a small gnawing worm.
Four empty dawns.[7]

I went to visit the Research Center for Art/Pottery after class yesterday. I was looking for something that was beautiful in the midst of all the destruction. The pottery is displayed in a lovely white room, with niches for each piece. The range is amazing, from coffee cups to waist-high vases. At the very top shelf there were three pieces that I couldn't identify: alabaster in color, a jar shaped like a rough grapefruit, a cup with an interior of old gold, and one piece that looked like a broken piece of brick or masonry. They were each marked with a small gold cross.

I was able to bring down the largest piece and open the lid. I was so startled by the contrast between the stark white and the interior of gold that I almost dropped the lid. I'm sure this is a eucharistic vessel, but it's so unusual. Now the smaller cup made sense, but what was the white piece that looked like a piece of rubble? I asked if it was for sale, or rather asked the student who was with me to ask if I could buy it. We were told to wait. She, by the way, is working on her doctoral thesis on Kant. Such smart, smart women in this place.

An older, very striking Korean man came into the room. He is the professor in charge of research design, and it was his work that I was looking at. He spoke no English but asked if I knew French. I replied that I only knew enough to say "No." He asked the student to translate.

It was a communion set, done in 1989. I asked him to explain the concept that he'd been working on, since the shapes were so puzzling. He picked up the small cup, placed it on top of the piece that looked like part of a broken wall. It was suddenly a chalice, but in a Korean style. He made this eucharistic set to celebrate the fall of the

Berlin Wall. He shows me the date that the wall went down. It's inscribed on the bottom. The broken masonry. The cup of forgiveness. He quotes something, and then says in English, "Ephesians."

For he himself is our peace,
Who has made the two one
And has destroyed the barrier,
The dividing wall of hostility . . . (Eph. 2:14 OEB)

White light goes off behind my eyes. Alabaster cups and cities gleam. The rubble from a wall of despair becomes a cornerstone. The vessel for Christ's body shaped like the round stone of a tomb or a human egg. The inside of each is painted with gold so pure it seems to cast light on my hand when I reach in.

I asked to buy it. I didn't care what it cost. Very expensive, he says. Yes. It will be worth it. There are very few things that can teach this kind of mystery. The price was 1,800,000 won (almost $1,500).

I nod; I say I'll be back tomorrow. I give him my card, tell him that I teach sacramental theology. I need this thing as a sign of healing, "an outward and visible sign of an inward invisible grace." This is the stuff of forgiveness, a love stronger than death. It gathers up the terrible images of the falling stones, the grey clouds, the burned bodies into this impossible piece/peace of Christ.

He's polite. Doesn't want to say no again. He offers to show me the kilns, the workroom. He's reluctant to show me a missing piece, the paten. "It is no good, it will need to be refired," he says. The gold is dull, dirty. The molten gold of the cup and the tarnished gold of the plate. It looks as if it's been stepped on. The gold of kings, the smudged print of the poor. I beg him again to let me buy it.

He's quiet for a few moments, then he asks the student to ask me something. "If he lets you buy this, will you promise to have everyone you show it to promise to pray that the walls between North and South Korea will come down." "On my honor," I say. "I'll ask them to pray."

He nods. It will be ready tomorrow. The price has changed. Only 200,000 won ($166). For he himself is our peace, who has made the two one. Please, please call.

September 21, 2001

What makes a wall fall down?
Start with the acts of God,
The earth moves. Mountains skip a beat.
Teutonic plates clash, crash together;
a rumble shapes the Rockies;
Atlantis sinks into unconsciousness.

Tornados, then.
Such suction pulls all sense
into the silent eye, the voiceless void.
Next, natural deconstruction:
Frost, wind, rain, sleet,
all hail breaks loose a stone, a brick, a beam.

Grave gravity, of course.
Entropy in fact
works patiently, so silently
as vertical turns horizontal.
Erectitude is softened to supinity.

Miracles come after.
A towering babble rises
as holy wrath descends.
Once upon a time a city's wall
comes tumbling, tumbling,
downed by trumpet sound.

Lastly, human hands.
A time to build up; a time to tear down.
A time to gather stones;
A time to shatter granite, scatter ash.
The tools of deconstruction:
picks, shovels, sledges,
cranes, crowbars,
(don't forget fingers)
and planes
Jesus! the planes . . .

bulldozing, flame throwing, steel-scorching
weapons of destruction.
Ashes to ashes. They all fall down.

O beautiful for patriot dream that sees beyond the years
thine alabaster cities gleam
undimmed by human tears!

What good is a fallen wall?
What survives where they, the hunters,
have left not one stone on a stone.
The fall of Berlin's wall broke down a war,
rearranged the board, rescued the pawns,
scrambled the stone cold lines.
Former foes, side by side, dig in the rubble for directions,
searching for home.

Perhaps it's come to this —
we old-stone savages need to lay our burdens down.

For he himself is our peace,
who has made the two one
and has destroyed the barrier,
the dividing wall of hostility . . .

Let Frost's Something take possession —
our apple orchards, amber waves,
and alabaster dreams.
We could be the crazy neighbors who un-fence our fathers' land;
take our stand beside the tower of ashy steel, and bone
and watch watch watch through the night
to see what kind of kin or alien
will cross this lamp-lit field to take our hand.[8]

three   THINGS THAT NAME THEMSELVES

Objects have biographies of their own, and it doesn't take a stretch of imagination to encounter some stuff, some thing that appears to be developing its own storyline. Poets, children, and practitioners of *homo reparans* often relate with things as subjects. The birth story of an object matters to the one who comes into possession of it, and the retelling of the story deepens the relationship between teller and thing and community. Sometimes the story of origin is so powerful it stimulates a rebirth in the teller and the community.

Objects certainly require human interpretation, but they can create, communicate, and embody sacredness. The consciousness of storytelling things is experienced in the improvised, yet intricate practices of religious life of ordinary people.[1] Ask any small gathering of people to tell you about what they would take if they had to evacuate or what Halloween costume they remember best and it will be clear that objects can have a social life and a network of relationships.[2]

I love my origin story of *pab sang po*, the Korean brightly colored quilted cloths that cover food. I found them at the farmers' market in Seoul. They say three things about love and food. First, if you see a table with food covered by the *pab sang po*, you know that the food is very fine. Second, whoever sets this table loves the one the meal is for. The third truth is that someone is waiting for her or his beloved to come. The food is being kept warm. The lover is waiting and the table is prepared. So ordinary yet sacramental.

Human consciousness is a process of binding things together; we have a genetic disposition to "grasp" life and make tangible connections with the embodied language of our senses and our bodily and psychological relationships with things. These "bound together" relationships are also the neural pathways for sacramental consciousness. Here are the verbal processing of sensed experience, ritual gestures, and the work of creating mental and material relationships. This process of binding, this consciousness of tangible connections, is at the center of our ceremonial life (from the Latin, *caerimonia*, to bind back together that which is separate). These are ceremonial stories that reflect consciousness of tangible connections between human stuff and holy life.

Those who hear me tell these stories are sometimes compelled to ask if I've made them up. The answer is no. I learned earlier on that my particular relationship to things requires that I pay close attention to them and say what I see. I interpret them as potential memory-makers, objects through which meaning can be made.

> Objects do not speak for themselves. They are interpreted.
> . . . As parables, objects made and used are not meant to be understood by all. They have hidden messages waiting for explanation, a fact that in itself holds a story. That story may come from connection to other objects and persons or from the perspective brought by stepping away from the situation.[3]

There's a selective side of storytelling, of course; one must chose to remember some things and forget others in order to frame a coherent narrative. Each of these narratives requires a suspension of disbelief or at least a sense of holy humor, but they are material witnesses to the work of the Spirit.

Another distinction to the narrative theology embedded in these stories is the assumption of the working of providence in strange and mysterious ways. The role of the Holy Spirit is primary. This emphasis on the third person of the Trinity is one of the hallmarks of Appalachian religion. As Deborah McCauley writes, "Grace and religious experience, mediated by the Holy Spirit, are at the core of this regional religious tradition. The individual is affirmed in the worshiping community through the autonomy of spontaneous self-expression, the integrity of which is valued by the group."[4] This expression of self is traditionally done as a story, a testimony, or a song, or if the calling came to preach, as a preaching style that stayed "close to the bone" in its use of personal narrative.

James Hopewell, using the work of Northrup Frye,[5] details structures of narrative in his book, *Congregations: Stories and Structures*, as the following:

> *Canonic:* This world view affirms an enduring and authoritative source of truth and life, usually understood to be the revealed will of God. To discern, trust, and obey is the desired response of the human to the Holy and provides narrative integrity.

> *Gnostic:* This world view affirms all reality is in the process of becoming one, moving from chaos to unity. As human wisdom deepens, brokenness, alienation, contradictions are understood to be temporary illusions. Integrity is achieved when all is seen as wholly One. The canonic claims of either/or are replaced by realizing both/and.

> *Charismatic:* This world view relies on "evidence of a transcendent spirit personally encountered. The integrity of providence in the world requires that empirical presumptions of an ordered world be disregarded and supernatural irregularities instead be witnessed."

> *Empiric:* This world view relies on a "prove it to me" approach. Reality must be empirically real, verifiable through one's own experience. Integrity is measured by practical standards and effective means; supernatural presumptions are rejected.[6]

The stories that follow can be read through the lens of two of the four forms of story: the canonical and charismatic are positioned as oppositional, but both maintain the necessity of transcendence. No single narrative structure can dominate the human imagination, and in the end the stories will mean what they will mean.

The Balm of Extra Virgin Cooking Oil

I AM A BAD COOK. I've often wondered if it was a matter of genes or culture, but since I've adapted to the defect, my husband shows no sign of defecting, and our son survived childhood, I feel as if the condition is probably permanent. I do note, in passing, that one of my son's favorite table graces had something to do with survival of the fittest. "Dear God, thank you for not making us dinosaurs. May we never be extinct."

From age nine to twelve, he attended St. Thomas Choir School in New York. It wasn't an easy fit. He wrote letters begging to come home every day for the first six months. The headmaster, Gordon Clem, would walk him to the mailbox every day. A wise heart master, he advised us, "Wait and see. Let the music do its work." A child would have to have an addiction to music to spend nineteen hours a week chanting psalms and singing like an angel, regardless of temperament.

It wasn't until Holy Week on his first year that his heart clearly spoke. The choir of men and boys have just finished singing St. Matthew's Passion. All the mothers are clustered around the stairs waiting to take their sons home. I watch our nine-year-old approach with a dazed look still in his eyes. He leans against my side and says, "That was more beautiful than life." I haven't had the heart to tell him that he'll probably end up being a Christian because of what he learned to sing by heart. I think it will kick in when he's about thirty.

At any rate, the school chef, who won blue ribbons regularly, would ask each new boy when he joined the school to bring in some of his mother's favorite recipes. Once or twice a month he would fix that boy's favorite dish as a cure for homesickness. It was a lovely practice that I never heard about until the choir school mothers decided to publish their recipe book. I received a very thoughtful call from the lead boy's mother asking if I didn't want to submit something other than what my son had turned in. Oodles of Noodles didn't quite fit the profile. We worked out a compromise. They included one of my poems instead of the noodles.

HANNAH AT ST. THOMAS

"Therefore I have lent him to the Lord . . ." 1 Samuel 1:28
In this madonna season I sit surrounded
by plain and not so plainsong,
searching for the one bright note attuned to my sound.
Like Hannah, I brave the eyebrowed skepticism
of presiding priests who rightly suspect
my presence is less pious,
more maternal.
No matter.
I know what I've laid on the altar.
Bone of bone.
Flesh of flesh.
A gift no usher could collect
in plates of silvered velvet.
In this madonna season I am reminded
that birth is just the first separation.
And though each sock is named,
each letter numbered,
there's a loss which is never reclaimed.
For each procession moves through time as well as space,
and every turn reveals less child, more power in his face.
Neither maestro nor messiah,
he simply lives and moves and sings.
And in place of angel visits,
I only ask
that in his dark of night
he'll hear
all that is holy call him by name. [7]

It should be clear from this account why I'm a great admirer of those who cook well. They reside in my imagination in the realms of the magical; wizards and mages, humans with supernatural powers to concoct marvels from basic compounds. When I make friends with good cooks I want to give them the best of the basics: stone ground flour, sea salt, kosher chicken broth, olive oil. I think what they do is like alchemy.

It was perfectly natural then to purchase a lovely bottle of extra virgin cooking oil for my former associate who'd been promoted to Registrar at his school. It was just accident that the shop was located in the train station in Rome. It was only a matter of timing that I bought it while waiting to join other pilgrims for an audience with the pope in the year of Jubilee. It fit neatly into my backpack, so off I went, well-anointed.

An audience with the pope is a good description, perhaps a little overstated when you remember that there are at least eight thousand other people also in the audience. But because the coteacher has impeccable connections, we have seats near the front, right on the center aisle. We can see him without the help of the giant screens.

He is frail, his hands tremble, but he delivers his greeting to us in five different languages. His text is from Genesis, and his address is as creative as his subject matter. At the end of the address, and after personally blessing at least fifty new brides and grooms dressed in their wedding best, he invites us, the audience, to bring out those things that we've brought for blessing. Here is the definitive difference between the households of Christ. We Protestants tend to minimize things, worried that their magnetic materiality might adhere to our souls, seduce us into idolatry. We put up rust-proof plaques. We don't ask to have things blessed for the length of "our lives, and for our children's children forever." But it doesn't take much convincing; everyone around me is pulling out things to be blessed, and I can see him coming down the center aisle.

I dig out the newly purchased bottle of extra virgin cooking oil. It's very biblical; there are over two hundred references to oil in the scriptures, most often olive oil. I hold it up and so it goes. Blessed for my children's children forever.

I think about it on the way home, unsure whether it's still a gift to be used for cooking. I get flashes from *Chocolat* and *Babbette's Feast*. What kind of a meal could you use this for without worrying your guests? The ecumenical implications are staggering.

I decide to shelve the bottle for a while. I have all the complexity I can handle at present. I'm flying back from a pilgrimage to Rome just in time to pick up a truckload of worship items for an event called "holy conferencing." It's an old-fashioned republican exercise of ecclesial politics. We hear reports and, in between, we elect bishops. We also have seventeen worship services and that's my "ministry beyond the local church," as they say.

We are picked up at the airport and I stuff my bags behind the front seat where all the communion elements are stored. We don't stop for a change of clothes, just drive directly to the conference center and start unpacking. The ancient glories of Rome are replaced by the heart-warming sounds of Wesleyans moving on to perfection.

The conference is coming to an end, and the ecclesial politics are heating up. There are several front runners. We have mixed feelings about the politics of competition, so this is "running" in the tradition of Philippians 3:13. Sixteen services down and one to go. I've had great help from two colleagues who treasure holy things and are very human people, but it's been a long week. We're glad to get to the one service I didn't have to design.

Holy Communion and consecration are the work of the bishops. My only task, and it's no small matter, is to provide the elements such as bread, grape juice (I know the word is "wine," but we don't indulge. Don't ask. It's a long story), crosses, candles, and the bulletins.

That last item is a very big deal. You have to have all the prayers, program notes, and a lovely wine-colored cover ready to go before the conference starts, but you can't print it until the Spirit moves and we elect a new bishop. That often happens in the early hours of the last day, so the printers get paid overtime. I rush to the phone, give the printers the name of the first African American woman elected bishop in this corner of the world and the ink starts flowing.

We're setting up the communion table when I get an additional assignment. Bishop Bashore is preaching and he wants to know if I happen to have a crozier. He didn't bring his. Since this is the big stick/shepherd's staff that only bishops carry, it's not an item I keep in stock in my holy hardware cupboard. He's disappointed. He really needs a staff because he's preaching the text of Exodus. Moses is stranded in the wilderness with this stiff-necked, impossible-to-please congregation. God tells him to hit the dry rock (instead of the hard-headed people) with his staff and, miracle of miracles, water begins to flood out of the rock and the people are saved. "I really need a staff, for the sermon, you see."

I did see. The necessity of a thing to make the Word right. I ask him if a real shepherd's staff might work. I have one from Scotland, not fancy, but functional. It even has a deer bone whistle that the shepherd can use to call for help if he gets stuck. Yes, he likes that idea. Get the staff. Now all I have to do is ask Bill to drive ninety miles before breakfast for the sake of a shepherd and his staff. God bless all long-suffering partners who have a sense of humor.

Everything is ready the next morning. It's 10:45 A.M., fifteen minutes to go. I check my list of holy things one last time as the people begin to gather and the bishops form a processional; bread and juice, cups and baskets, processional cross and a Scottish shepherd's staff. The wine-colored worship programs have just arrived; the ink still damp. My delight in reading a woman's name, Violet Fisher, beside the title, Shepherd of the Church, is as permanent as the ink.

I turn to check on the candles, and we plunge into darkness. All the power is out. We're in the literal dark. The surprised laughs that mask anxiety keep us energized for several minutes, and then the hotel officials arrive with flashlight and an ultimatum: everyone leaves, now. It's the rule. We can't take our purses, or any of our worship material. We must leave now, and leave we do, led by our bishops, moving slowly through the darkened hallways into the light of the outer courtyard.

The Holy One has a strange sense of order as well as humor. Here we are, eight hundred more or less would-be worshipers herded out on the grass while everything we need to consecrate a bishop is locked inside. Those of us in robes confer, but we're without a clue as to what to do except wait until the power returns.

Mark Miller, the minister of music, leads the others in singing. Watches are checked as fervently as prayer beads. The hotel is only reserved until 1 P.M. The service usually lasts two hours. We can't go home until a bishop is consecrated.

I start inspecting the small lake beside the hotel for liturgical possibilities. There's a deck built out on the water. It looks like it might hold all the bishops and the prie-dieu where a bishop traditionally kneels to be consecrated. We can place the elements in baskets and cups at the edge of the lake. People could simply crowd around the shoreline.

It's now 11:15. Time to improvise. The hotel managers are getting worried about eight hundred stranded United Methodists who won't leave until something sacred happens. Two of the tallest bishops go to talk with the managers. Authority needs a little altitude as well as attitude. They request that they and I be allowed to retrieve the communion elements, the prayer kneeler, and the bulletins.

The management is reluctant, it breaks the fire code rules to let us back in a powerless building, but they sense a looming disaster, and agree. Using flashlights, we round up the basic necessities for worship, including the shepherd's staff. I even bring out the box stuffed with the extra bread (and my unpacked box from Rome) just in case we run out.

We set up to serve communion and consecrate in the great outdoors. The bishops arrange themselves on the dock. It's the floating kind, so there's a little caution about not clumping together at the edges. The elements are ready, the bulletins handed out, the kneeler's in place, the service begins, and the sky starts to darken.

I notice, but assume the Almighty has provided us with all the freedom and free fall we can handle for the day. I'm on the deck with the bishops to provide whatever service is needed. Since it's been weeks since I've looked at the service notes, I'm as surprised as the others to hear the gospel text that's being read. "That same day Jesus went out of the house and sat beside the sea. Such great crowds gathered around him that he got into a boat and sat there, while the whole crowd stood on the shore . . ." I can see the grins growing as the reading goes on and one of my former bishops, William Boyd Grove, edges over to where I'm standing and whispers, "If you wanted to hold this service outside, why didn't you just ask us?"

This isn't my fault. I'm in sales, not management, as least when it comes to prayer and the weather, but I'm beginning to hope someone else on deck is in upper management. The sky has gone from dull blue to grey to thundercloud black in less than twenty minutes. The sermon has begun, and Bishop Bashore is using both the text and the staff in a very effective manner. He is, in fact, preaching up a storm. People are starting to look up, but more perplexed than pious. We're locked out of the hotel, it looks like rain, and we have to consecrate a bishop before we can go home.

The bishop is gathering energy up like a lighting rod. Moses is at the rock. The people have pushed Moses and God too far and now, God help us, he's lifting the staff. Moses and the bishop. He's getting ready to strike the rock. We all know what happens next. The first rain drops begin to fall. The bishop doesn't notice. The wind picks up. He raises his arm, holding the rod in his fist. Someone on the shore gets carried away, and shouts, "Don't strike the rock!"

Too late. He brings the staff down in his palm with a sharp smack and the skies break open. Water, water, everywhere. It's not raining, it's pouring. It's not a shower, it's a deluge. The communion bread is soaked in seconds; the cups fill and start overflowing. There's no place to take shelter. When I think it can't get worse, I see people trying to keep the rain off with their brand-new worship bulletins and the lovely wine-colored covers have turned into streams of permanent ink, staining hands and heads as it flows. It looks as if we're being washed in the blood of the lamb.

Desperation drives us all into the lobby where there's still no power. Some have given up and made a dash for their cars. The management agrees to let us stay until we get done whatever we need to do. What on earth is possible? The ink has run on the bulletins, the baskets of bread are awash. There's not enough extra bread in the soaked cardboard box to start over and I don't know where the cups have gone.

We set up the kneeler in front of the front desk in the lobby and the bishops try to wring out their albs. Just a consecration, then, but wait . . . at the heart of every baptism is an anointing with oil, a sealing by the Spirit. If we can't celebrate communion, we'll renew our baptism.

I just happen to have holy oil, blessed by the pope in a wilted cardboard box that's sitting under a table in the lobby. I go to the resident bishop with my flash of inspiration. Let's renew our baptism. We're certainly well immersed, wet behind the ears. "I have," I tell him without blinking an eye, "holy oil. It's blessed by the pope." He knows me well enough to know that I'm serious. I decide it's not necessary to tell him that this started out as extra virgin cooking oil. I have no idea what the sacramental reality is going to be if we use pope-blessed oil on the foreheads of United Methodists for baptismal renewal, particularly in a service for a woman who will be consecrated bishop. I ignore the proverb about mixing oil and water and go in search of glasses.

I decide to let the oil speak for itself. It has its own narrative line, rising from the pages of scripture and practices of tradition. "Thou anointest my head with oil" sang the psalmist. Its presence is a holy human relationship as deep and wide as the mercy of God.

A renewal of baptism, then. I pour extra virgin cooking oil into the shot glasses that Mark Conner and Stacy Douglas, two enterprising liturgists in their own right, have borrowed from the hotel bar.

The bishops form a ring around the new bishop and lead her to the kneeler. I'm standing with my back against the front desk, the little shot glasses lined up to hand each bishop after they finish laying hands on Violet's head and consecrating her. They will then take the glass of oil and sign the cross on the foreheads of the newly washed believers and remind them to remember their baptism and be thankful.

Just as the oldest bishop, who will bless her first, lifts his hands to invoke the Spirit, all the power snaps back on. We've got light, we've got air conditioning, and we've got phones ringing off the hook. The woman behind the front desk quickly crosses herself and turns off the phones. I don't know if she knows what we're doing, but she isn't going to let business get in the way.

We've got the power; we've also got company. The rain has stopped, and two new groups start coming in the front doors of the lobby where there are very wet Christians doing some strange ritual. The first through the door are the Beer Drinkers of America, carrying in display boards and kegs. Right behind them is the second group, competitors in a cat show. They're carrying cages of cats. Cats and beer and extra virgin cooking oil blessed by the pope swirling around in a hotel lobby. Bishop Fisher couldn't have asked for a better site for her consecration.

My favorite image for heaven was formed that day in a hotel lobby watching Bishop Irons make the sign of the cross using extra virgin cooking oil blessed by the pope on the forehead of some woman holding a cat in a cage. Maybe she thought it was some new way to check into the hotel or maybe she knew exactly what was going on and wanted in on the blessing. After all, it's for our children and for our children's children forever.

The Sparrow Tattoo

READING MY EMPLOYMENT HISTORY, one might think I suffer from attention deficit disorder (ADD). I do a little of this, a little of that, and now for something completely different . . . I've never lived longer than four years in one home, and I've just been moved into the ninth office inside the same building I've worked in for more than fifteen years. There was one job I held for two years that I plan to return to when I retire: truck-stop chaplain. I've kept the plastic name tag so I won't have to order a new one.

The committee that hired me wouldn't have if another applicant had applied. I wouldn't have applied if I could have gotten hired in a respectable job, such as Christian educator. But we'd moved to a new conference, and no one cared about my eight years of parish ministry plus three years as a university chaplain. I was a pastor's wife, attending school part-time. So my desperation to pay for tuition and their desperation to use the grant money they'd received for this position meshed very nicely.

They gave me a plastic name tag, "Truck-stop Chaplain," and a sign that read: "Chaplain is in." I was to put the sign on the cash register at the front whenever I came to work. I was to put the name tag on a black suit with a clergy collar. They wanted to be very sure that the truckers could distinguish me from the other women who might be looking for work there.

Every night was new, each encounter different. I got good at consuming coffee and listening hard, swallowing smoke and learning about the best way to drive in snow, hanging out with the waitresses on their breaks, and writing blessings on napkins. These were the traveling mercy nights and what I learned has taken me a long way toward home. But there's one story that got under my skin; there's one memory I'm marked with for as long as I can remember.

He's stirring his coffee when I sit down beside him at the counter. The men and women who drive usually sit at the counter when they're being fueled if they're not too tired, or behind in their paperwork. So I sit beside him on a stool, and I notice that he doesn't even turn his head. Sometimes it means that he sees me, dressed all in black with a white collar and doesn't know what to make of me. A guy asked me once if I was "one of those women who married God for life?" I told him no, that I belonged to the people who believed in long engagements.

Sometimes they don't look at me because they are shy or they want me to go away. Since I never know until I ask, I look for a way to open up a conversation. I notice that he's still stirring his coffee and that he has a braided tattoo like a bracelet around his wrist.

Start with the obvious. It must mean something. So I ask about what it means, this braided tattoo. It turns out that he was in the navy; it's a navy thing. He falls silent and I look for another door. I've never gotten a tattoo, I say. Did it hurt to get this one? "Nah," he shook his head, "not that one. But this one," and here he pushes up his left sleeve so I can see his arm, "this one hurt like . . ." he notices what I'm wearing, "this one hurt a whole lot."

I nod. It would have. It covers most of his upper arm, and the skin on the edges is still puffy and red. I study the tattoo. It's done in three colors, very precise, but it's not quite what I imagined a trucker to wear. It's flowers and a bird of some kind, with outspread wings. I ask him what kind of bird it was. He stares at it for several moments and then says, "I dunno, some kind of sparrow, I think."

His confusion makes me very curious. Since most folks in a truck stop are just passing through, conversations tend to be direct. If you're on the road, you might as well say what you think and move on. So I say, "You don't even know what kind of bird that is. Why did you get that tattoo?"

His reason had something to do with an older tattoo. Could I tell there's a woman's name under the bird's wings? I could make out the faint letter "S." "You see," he said, "once I dated a girl named Sue. I got her name tattooed on my arm just before I shipped out. When I got out, I got married, but I didn't marry Sue. My wife hated my left arm for eighteen years so I fixed it."

He studies the new three-color tattoo like he's seeing it for the first time. I'm processing what I've heard. Eighteen years. Why fix it now? I ask as soon as the thought crosses my mind.

He stirs his coffee again and then begins the story of the origin of his winged tattoo. He was a steel worker, third generation. He was doing well, working hard on keeping up with family and financial obligations. A strike was called; it lasted over two years and when it ended the plant was permanently closed. He'd been so sure that all he had to do was hang on, find part time work until they called him back. His sense of worth shrank as the debts mounted. He took whatever day job was open, but the massive layoff meant there was little left open for full-time work. His wife took a night job at Wal-Mart and he watched the kids.

Then, he said, something changed. First, for the worse. They were behind in their mortgage, the utilities unpaid. One of the kids ended up in the hospital, but there was no insurance, so the doctors came first. Bottom-line economics. He came across a trucking brochure advertising eighteen-wheelers for owner/operators. Buy your own truck complete with driver's training. All he needed was ten thousand dollars for a down payment.

That's more than a dollar and a dream. How did he manage? "You know," he's talking faster now, eager to explain, "that's a lot of money, but I got this feeling that," and he stops, lowers his voice and gestures upward with his thumb, "You Know Who sent it."

I shake my head to clear it. It's nearly two in the morning and I've had too much caffeine. "You know who?" He nods again and gestures heavenward. "God? You mean you thought God sent you the brochure?" "Yeah," he said. "Him."

I'm wide awake now and fascinated. I have no idea how this connects with a brand-new tattoo, but I'm intrigued by someone who won't say "God." Since I hear the Second Commandment broken on a minute by minute basis, his hesitation makes his story one of a kind. "What did you do, since God sent it?"

He made a list of ten people, friends who could each lend him a thousand dollars. He'd sign notes, get the truck, get on the road, and pay them back in six months. "How did it go?"

"Not good. I'd have quit if I didn't think," the thumb gesture again, "you know, sent it. I got to number nine and they'd all turned me down."

"Then . . ." I prompt. "Then the last guy gave me every last penny I needed." I blink, take a breath. "That's a miracle!" He's back to stirring his coffee, doesn't look up. I retrace my steps. "Why isn't that a miracle?"

It is, but not right away. He takes the money to the bank, asks to see the loan officer, puts the filled out loan form and the cash on the desk. "I'm here to buy my truck. Here's the down payment." The officer looks at his form, checks his credit rating and turns him down. He asks why. His credit rating is lousy. End of story.

"I try to explain. Tell them I want to work. I'm a hard worker. If they loan me the money, I'll be able to work and my credit will be good again. They just keep saying they're sorry, but my credit rating is lousy. I get mad, then I apologize. I beg to talk with the bank president. They tell me the interview is over."

"So I go home and wake my wife up, and we sit on the couch and hold hands and I say a . . ." here he begins to fumble his words, "I say a kind of a . . . I say . . ." "You say a prayer." I finish his sentence. "Yeah, I say one of those." My amazement keeps growing at the notion of a language too holy to use in everyday speech.

"What did you say?" "I said, 'If it was supposed to happen, could it happen, please? Amen.'" A pretty good prayer, come to think of it. "Nevertheless, not my will . . ." "Go on." "Well, then it got really crazy. In about twenty minutes, my neighbor knocks on the door with the news that the bank just called them and I'm supposed to call them back right away. I had to give them my neighbor's number because they'd cut off our phone. So I call the bank, and they tell me to come back and bring the money. I can have the loan and buy my truck."

Now I stir my coffee to hide the quick flash of tears. "That is a miracle." He doesn't respond, so I try again. "Wasn't that a miracle?"

"Here's my problem." He's talking fast again, but avoids my eyes. "I make good money now. The house is paid for; my loan's paid off. I can get my kids what they need to look good. She doesn't have to work at Wal-Mart anymore. But to do this means I'm on the road twenty-five days every month. I get home and they don't know me and I'm so tired I don't care. She thinks I don't love her anymore and I don't know what she thinks about me. You get road fever in this job. It gets so hard to go home; after a while you keep driving."

"I've got road fever. I can feel it getting stronger. So this morning I pull my rig over when I see a tattoo sign and I go in and tell the guy to fix this arm. Whatever it takes. Now I'm going to head home and try to show her. I don't want it to be over."

He's turned his stool so we're nearly face to face. "Do you think . . ." He looks away, then tries again, "Do you think God cares about stuff like this?" I say my own kind of prayer. Please. Please. Give me the right words. "God cares . . ." His head jerks around. They're reading his number over the speakers. He's fueled and has to get moving. He picks up his bill from the counter.

I start talking, fast. "Do you have a Bible?" "No," he says. I follow him to the cash register. "Would you take a Bible? They're free. We give them away." He hesitates. "Take a Bible and when you get where you're going, open it up and look for the name Matthew. It's a little book toward the back." "Matthew, like a man's name?" I hand him a Bible. "Yes. Read Matthew. It has the answer to your question. What God cares about."

"What's the answer?" He's flipping through the pages, wondering if I'm putting him on. "You'll have to find it. It's there. It's got your name on it." "So how will I know when I find it?" "You'll know when you find the word 'sparrow.' You'll see what that tattoo really means, what kind of permanent mark God just made on your life."

"A sparrow?" "Yes, there's a promise about sparrows in the gospel called Matthew."

I watch him walk out with the Bible tucked under his decorated left arm. I never see him again. I don't know if he reads it, or if love turns out to be the real miracle story after all. What I do know is this, as the years pass, and I start to despair about the sparrows that are falling, falling, falling, the good news I offered to him sometimes returns to me. "Don't be afraid. You are worth more than the sparrows."

The Dead Christmas Tree

TO REDEEM: ▪ buy back, recover by expenditure of effort or by a stipulated payment ▪ make a single payment to discharge ▪ convert into goods or cash ▪ (of God and Christ) deliver from sin and damnation ▪ make up for; be a compensating factor in ▪ save from ▪ purchase the freedom of a person ▪ fulfill a promise

For as the rain and snow come down from heaven,
and do not return there until they have watered the earth,
making it bring forth and sprout,
giving seed to the sower and bread to the eater,
so shall my word be that goes out from my mouth;
It shall not return to me empty,
but it shall accomplish that which I purpose,
and succeed in the thing for which I sent it.
For you shall go out in joy,
and be led back in peace;
The mountains and the hills before you shall burst into song,
and all the trees of the field shall clap their hands.
Instead of the thorn shall come up the cypress
instead of the brier shall come up the myrtle;
and it shall be to the LORD for a memorial,
for an everlasting sign that shall not be cut off. (Isa. 55:10–13)

IMAGINE. Just imagine: a mass of humanity, staggering under the weight of horrendous loss, stripped of the basic comforts of life and the simple dignity of being human, forcibly ripped by the roots from their ground of being, families torn apart, children without parents, the old without the young. Their neighborhoods, their possessions are shattered; the stench of death is everywhere. All the foundations have been washed away, and their memories scattered like flood debris. They're homeless, strangers in a strange land, forced into shadows and servitude of a superpower that sees them as alien, foolish, and weak.

"Surely," say the empire's religious leaders, "surely their deity has deserted them. This is the work of an angry God, a just punishment for their stiff-necked sins." Once they were treasured. Now they are trash.

You don't need to imagine, do you? Just turn on the TV or walk outside. Earthquakes, hurricanes, tsunamis, and famines have made the stories of human suffering so familiar that we don't need to imagine what the community of the unknown singer/poet we call Isaiah was experiencing. We don't need to imagine their context. We hear echoes of their cries in the words of the unknown prophet. I suggest that we should commit this text to memory. We need to know this one by heart.

Here are the weary ones of exile, trapped in vicious cycles of violence and slavery, living hand to mouth and day to day. Their lives are crushed by the power of random evil. They are trapped in a living death and are starving for hope, thirsting for a word that will quench despair. This is the context of their life and this text.

Now imagine, just imagine. Someone rises and begins to sing. Here is the tongue of one who is taught, here is the sound of a wonderful counselor who knows how to console the weary with a word in the morning. Here is someone whose language and life summons a new world into view.

For you shall go out in joy,
    and be led back in peace;
The mountains and the hills before you shall burst into song,
    and all the trees of the field shall clap their hands.

Surely it would be sufficient to simply read these words aloud. Isn't Christ truly present in the reading and the hearing of the Word? Musicians will hear a hundred favorite anthems in these lines and preachers resonate to the dream of a common language, a whole and holy word that will raise the quick and the dead. Soon and very soon a great thanksgiving will be set in motion that calls together the communion of saints, the unborn, the reborn, those who have been, those who will be, and all the company of heaven. Incline your ears and come. Listen, and live.

Imagine being part of a song so potent that deep harmonics of your being begin to resonate with creation itself and all the morning stars and the daughters and sons of God sing for joy. Imagine a sound so deep that you'll see the blasted mountains rise again and the sewage-filled valleys go sweet and green before your very eyes.

Imagine. Just imagine a Word sent out into creation, a prophetic utterance that clears the ground of an ancient curse, and transforms the toxic waste of war into a memorial garden. There will be fields as far as the eye can see free of the kudzu of greed and the multiflora thorns of hate.

Imagine: A table of rich food that delights us like the first taste of chocolate and yet, here's the real miracle, we only eat what's good. A cup of living water that quenches our thirst and cures our addiction. It's a cuisine that's not lean, a meal that heals our ulcerated appetites, and it tastes divine.

And who's invited? Isaiah reminds us that it's the promise breakers, the liars, the spin doctors, the talking heads, the false prophets, the thought police, preachers of sound and fury whose words signify nothing, those who fear to break the silence of oppression, those who hunger to have their life and their language redeemed. Here's where God's poetic prophet names what is definitely not visible, the commonwealth of God, the place where Forever begins.

Here's the prophetic utterance that, as J. L. Austin puts it, performs the reality it names. Hear—right here—the sound of life and language becoming one: freedom, space, breathing room, energy, power, and the ability to love, the death of death, and the circle of life. Just imagine.

Why would I use an ambiguous verb like "imagine"? It's elusive, hard to diagram, has a controversial history if the Re-imagining Conference is any indication. Why would I want to use a word that risks self-deception, a word that means "to invent, to make up."

I found the answer this summer in David Kelsey's little book *Imagining Redemption*.[8] When you have to move home and office in the same summer, you begin to question the value of these things called books, particularly when they number in the thousands. You begin to ask yourself, "Was this really worth the life of a tree?" In this case, *Imagining Redemption* is worth the sacrifice because it's written by someone who knows that forgiveness of sins can save your life. It's worth the sacrifice because it's the failure of imagination that plagues preaching and it's our addiction to despair that resists redemption.

I remind myself how easy it is to fall into the temptation of a failed imagination. My husband and I were visiting England on a parish exchange and we were invited for tea at the home of a church superintendent and his wife. All salaries are equal in the English Methodist system, so few who retire can afford to buy their own homes. Consequently, many finish their life work in Preachers' Homes. The superintendent was showing my husband, Bill, some of the very good choices of Homes that they were considering. I noted that his wife was having none of it. I tried to say something innocuous, like "It must be hard to resettle at the end . . ." or something to that effect. "Oh, no," she said, "That's not the problem. I'm used to moving. But can you imagine having to grow old surrounded by people who think that life is an occasion for sermons?"

Back to the verb: imagine. It means "to grasp a concrete particular as some kind of whole." What concrete particulars of ordinary life might be redeemable? Is there redemptive stuff that can help us grasp the mysterious love of the One who creates and sustains us?

1) To redeem (or re-deem): to make up for a bad performance. God redeems human history through the life, passion, death, and resurrection of the Beloved. Just imagine: a tree is turned into an instrument of torture. It becomes the matter of atonement. An object of humiliation becomes a tree of life.

2) To redeem: to regain possession of something that has been sold into slavery or to free something from alien control. To redeem our imagination means that we regain possession of something that has been pawned: It's an example of alien possession if we, who

were left high and dry, declare hurricanes were sent to wash a city clean of the poor and the old and the stubborn and the sinful. Those of us who dare to ask: "Is there a word?" need to remember the Holy One's answer: "Your ways are not my ways, and your thoughts not my thoughts."

Redeem means that a promise is made good. Think about the deep green power of the Word that is scattered into creation, the nearly scandalous generosity of God who sows life with a wide, wild throw. God has promised; the Word is sent into the world to work the will of the Sower, the Sender, and the Spirit. This kind of promise, this kind of language, God's and ours, has the power to create something new. The promise made in Jesus has the power to call a new creation into being, and that power/promise/relationship includes each and all. That's efficacy. That's stuff so potent it can create a greening of life and language. That's an act of imagination and redemption that makes mountains sing and trees clap their hands.

Let me tell you a story about a boy from the mountains and a tree.

I paid a visit to a former parsonage recently. I wanted to see if a blue spruce was still planted in the yard of Tranquility UMC, where only the dead are at peace. Once there were two trees, now only one. They were planted the same year, our first Christmas in New Jersey. It was my son's idea, his demand, really. He'd gotten the strangest notion that nothing should die at Christmas. So we buy two trees, one for him, one for my nephew who'd come to live with us.

I had a notion why my seven-year-old fixated on live trees. He's been forcibly uprooted from the hills of Almost Heaven, carried into pastoral exile if you will. He doesn't transplant well, and his roots aren't holding. When I ask him why he couldn't try to be happy in the Garden State, he looks away and tells me that I didn't pack his heart and you can't be happy without a heart.

I see almost as soon as he says it a young green life begin to shrivel up and die, defeated by the rocky ground.

He wants a real tree for Christmas. We purchase two, one for him, one for my nephew, who also needs grounding. We decorate, celebrate, prepare the ground, transplant according to directions, and right in the front yard, without permission from the trustees. We wanted, needed to see redemption every morning. One rooted. One didn't. One reached for the sun. One began to get brittle. One started living and one began to die. Which one? The one my son had chosen.

He doesn't give up easily. He talks to the tree while he waits in the yard for the school bus. Maybe he's praying. That's what I'm doing, watching him watch that tree. We think about digging it up in the middle of the night and replacing it. Fear of making it worse stops us cold. The tree turns yellow and then brown and we don't talk about it.

I find him in the attic one morning digging in the Christmas things. He wants an ornament. Why? So it might remember what it was supposed to be, a Christmas tree. So now there's one dead tree in the yard with a silver ornament tied with a scarlet ribbon. One tree of life and one dead Christmas tree, one child who is reaching for the stars, and one who is taking less and less space.

In the midst of this living death I was asked to do the Bible study for a youth conference. It was going to be a Bible study from hell: fifty-plus minutes, for four days, with five thousand teenagers packed into an un-air-conditioned gym. I need help. I'm working on the parable of the sower because we are going to be in the middle of America's heartland, surrounded by field of corn. I need help with the rocky ground part because that's where I am. The Word has me in a stranglehold and isn't giving an inch.

I ask our son if I can tell the kids about his tree. I think it might help some of them to grasp the stone-cold truth that sometimes love can't keep those we love alive. There are parts of the Sower story that should break our hearts.

He agrees that I need help. "You're not very good with kids," he says and I agree. I need help. He walks away, and then reappears a few minutes later, dragging the shovel. "Let's show them. Kids don't listen to just talking." I'm following in his footsteps, more than perplexed about this word/act that's taking place. He starts digging. "You can take it with you. Show them." I'm thinking about the airport, the mess, the explanation. I keep quiet and help him dig. At least it will get the tree out of the front yard.

It takes a very large plastic bag to transport the tree, roots and all. I decide to put it in the car and have Bill drop it into a trash bin after he drops me off at the airport. Daniel decides to ride with the tree, see it off on its journey. I'm still thinking, "Very big trash bin, inside the terminal" when I climb out. But that dies a quick death when he assures me, "Now it feels like it counted for something."

So it is. So it goes. I drag a suitcase and a very large black plastic bag into the security line. What happens next is a story that will never happen again, not in the lifetime of Homeland Security.

I lay the plastic bag down on the belt and start praying. It gets half way through the machine and the uniformed guard punches the stop button. She's peering at her screen and then at me.

"What *is* that thing?"

I check the scanner. "An ornament, a decoration."

"And what else?" She demands, "What in the world have you got in this bag?"

I pause.

"A dead Christmas tree."

I've no idea why she let me get onto the plane. At least I didn't have to buy it a ticket.

So we arrive, tree and me, in the middle of Kansas. I begin my first Bible study, the parable of the sower, and the tree saves my life. They listen, fascinated by the weirdest show-and-tell they've seen a grown-up do. We talk about how hard some parts of the story are. I tell them, show them, that sometimes love isn't enough to keep someone alive. At the end of the teaching, I invite the crisis counselor to join me. I give him the tree and invite any one who's lost someone they loved to come and visit the tree.

At the end of the day he finds me and asks, "Did you want that tree back again?" "No, once was enough," I assure him. "Good," he said, "Because it's all gone. I gave it away." He tells me about the crisis center being packed with people, mostly young, but not all. So he had them say their name and who they had lost, and how they felt. When all the talking was done, he invited everyone who wanted to touch the tree and take a piece to remember that love makes a difference in life and death and life beyond death. "They took it all, piece by piece, even the roots. I gave a twelve-year-old who'd lost her mother the ornament."

Imagine. Just imagine. The Word goes out, and on its way home, it brings a promise of green.

Five years later, I'm doing a youth service in Dallas. I've gotten a little better with kids. I'm in a circle of kids just after the service, talking and laughing, and listening. I see a tall young man at the edge of the circle wave his arms to get my attention. I look at him and nod and then he takes something from his shirt pocket and holds it up. It's a twig, a dried piece of pine. He shouts across the distance, "Tell him it made a difference!" Imagine. Just imagine. The Word goes out, and on its way home, it brings a promise of green. You know, for just a moment, I thought I heard the sound of clapping.

four   STUFF FOR REPAIRING THE WORLD

A thing is a thing is a thing. But add a story, and it is transformed in front of our eyes. The same object can sustain multiple meanings and even opposing narratives. It can inhabit structures of meaning that shift only slightly as we age, like a foundation that settles. It can collapse like a levy, flooding us with chaos and suffering.

A story is an invitation to cross a threshold, to enter a space where the tyranny of time is held at bay. It can also be the trapdoor to an abyss where nothing survives, not even memory. We sustain this destruction of meaning in the hope that some new life will emerge from the wreckage. We tell stories as a means of sanctifying time, redeeming things, and repairing relationships. We surround ourselves with stuff that matters. We tell stories about things as a means of remembering who we were, and are, and will be in the future.

We are creatures who want to repair and restore the world we inhabit.[1] The evidence is everywhere. I have a hand-carved wooden scoop hanging on my wall. It's walnut, probably used for measuring out the grain in a barn. What's striking about it is the split up the middle and what someone did about it. Two hand-hammered staples hold the tool together and keep it useful. Someone made it.

Someone repaired it. Someone else preserved what had been done. Someone else tells a story about what it means.

This is *bricolage*. The word comes from the French word for janitor, or someone who is handy at doing repairs.

> It uses a limited, heterogeneous repertoire of inherited bits and pieces. It makes do with whatever is at hand, with a set of tools and materials which is always finite and is also heterogeneous because what it contains bears no relation to the current project, or indeed to any particular project, but is the contingent result of all the occasions there have been to renew or enrich the stock or to maintain it with the remains of previous constructions or destructions.[2]

This chapter of stories has "made do with whatever is at hand." There are pieces of scriptural interpretation hardwired into personal stories. These are stories filled with stuff that helped to form relationships or marked their demise, made life a little more human or harder than it needs to be.

A Piece of the Rock

THE GROOM WAS REALLY LATE. The bride had begun to cry and her father was breaking the Second Commandment in the doorway of the church. I could hear the screeching of tires, followed by brakes, and a door slamming that signaled all was not lost. He launched himself into the sanctuary, tux awry and badly stained at the knees. He was talking nonstop and holding a sharp edged rock in his hand. It was his evidence, his witness, his excuse, his hope for forgiveness.

He'd forgotten the rings. He'd forgotten to give them to the best man. He only remembered when he was halfway to church. He'd turned around; he had plenty of time to make the thirty-minute drive to church. But he hadn't counted on backing over something that punctured his front tire right in his own driveway. He held the rock out like a prayer.

He'd had to change the tire, ruined his tux, upset his bride to be, and made his future father-in-law very unhappy. It was all the rock's fault. We reorganized the ceremony, dried tears, tried to remove oil stains, and a good time was finally had by all.

On the first anniversary of their wedding, he was served breakfast in bed by his wife who kept trying not to grin. He discovered why when he encountered the rock in the bottom of his coffee cup. The next year, she was the one surprised with a brand new hiding place. As far as I know, they're still married and engaged in this curious exchange. It's their peace of the Rock. They repair their relationship year by year with humor and memory. They have the right stuff.

Liturgy Is the Work of the People

ASH WEDNESDAY

Christmas had come and gone, neatly packed for another year. Epiphany had been duly celebrated with a baptism and songs about starry-eyed travelers. Ordinary time provided a little breathing room. "Ash Wednesday" was circled on my calendar in purple ink. I flipped through the bulletin files of my predecessors preserved in the universally gray filing cabinets. There were random samples of Palm Sunday, Maundy Thursday, Good Friday, and an Easter bulletin collection from 1928 to the present. No sign of Ash Wednesday, however.

Why? I ask the saints in this particular corner of the kingdom. They don't try to hide their surprise at the question. I get the same answer each time I ask. It points out how much I have to learn about Christianity 101 in this corner of the world. "That's what Catholics do."

Their matter-of-factness makes me pause. In a small Appalachian river town with a telephone directory that reads like the United Nations, the line between a Protestant and Catholic isn't exactly drawn in invisible ink. Who you have coffee with is one thing; who your daughter dates is another. Once a year, the line between neighbors is drawn in ash. Some have the sign; others don't. You don't cross the line.

I've been raised to cross lines. Some crossings are needed so that we can mean what we say when we recite the Apostle's Creed. We don't have to sing in the same key or pray the same way for Jesus to recognize that we're part of the family. Irreducible diversity in unity is at the heart of the mystery of the Trinity. I also know that Lent is the start of the story of Amazing Grace and that story starts with a heap of ashes.

The smudge line between Us and Them is only one of the barriers we'd have to cross to retrieve the practice of the apostolic church in this congregation. No ashes, therefore no Ash Wednesday, plus they celebrate Palm Sunday minus palms. No palms to make ashes. The reason I'm given is economics, not ecumenics. "We can't afford the greenery." I know part of this story from experience. They couldn't/ didn't pay my salary for almost two months. They did, however, keep us well fed. I've noticed that flowers appear in the bulletin for Mother's Day and Christmas, and even a modest number of lilies for Easter, but the classic Christian way to tell time organically from Lent to Lent is missing.

I circle Ash Wednesday again on my calendar. I prepare a way for us to learn to tell time like Christians in this time and place. We study all the passages in the Bible that refer to ashes during our Wednesday night prayer service. Ashes to ashes. Dust to dust. The refrain keeps working its way deeper into my brain.

I make a hospital visit just after Christmas. A miner is dying of black lung, death from the dark diamonds of coal. I walk by the gift shop on the way to the elevator when I see a figure carved out of coal on the sale table. I take a quick detour. It's calling my name. It's the figure of an old woman, made out of coal. She's sitting, her apron filled with fruit. She's offering to sell it or give it away. I think about our depleted checking account and tell myself that if it costs more than twenty-five dollars, I need to put it down and walk away quickly.

I turn her over and smile. The sale price is five dollars. I'm staring at the difference between art and just "stuff." The sales woman has spotted me, thinks I need encouragement. "I can let you have that for $2.50. It's not really carved, you see. It's just coal dust glued together.

Coal dust glued together. What are people from the mineral-rich mountains but coal dust glued together? We wear black diamonds on our shoes, and in our souls and bodies. Mountains are being leveled and dumped into streams for the sake of this stuff. Towns are made and destroyed by management decisions. Life-sustaining jobs keep shrinking as the machines get bigger. Most of the profit ends up in out-of state pockets. But what other work is there for people to do?

I walk the train tracks and wander the streets of the town tucked between the hills and the river, picking up random pieces of coal that have fallen off the coal trains. When I'm asked what I'm doing I tell them I'm working on worship.

Ash Wednesday arrives. They're invited to a simple supper of soup and bread prepared by the Sunshine class in the Fellowship Hall. "Sixteen Tons" and other coal mining songs play in the background during supper. We sing old-time gospel songs. I tell them I have a gift of coal dust to give them. I know what it means. The miner I visited in the hospital explains it to me as he struggles to breathe after spitting up part of his lung. "That's coal for you. It goes in dark as sin and comes out the color of blood." Every breath reminds me we are dust.

Most of them come to the altar. I hand the lay leader the bowl of coal dust and kneel. He marks me and then kneels for his own sign of death and life and Lent. He rises and others take his place. Mixed in with the soft swell of the organ is the sound of people weeping.

PALM SUNDAY

I've discovered a florist hidden in the church rolls. He never attends; I invite him, but he looks away and says "It's hard to explain." He won't budge beyond that but clearly wants a way out of his seeming resistance. I ask the price of palm branches. By the time we've finished this curious nonconfession and assurance of acceptance, he's agreed to donate palm branches in memory of his father.

The children learn to make crosses out of the leaves. They show the grownups how when Palm Sunday comes. They promise to remember. As I visit through the next year I see the drying palm crosses in Bibles, on kitchen shelves, even over a tool table.

MAUNDY THURSDAY

Foot washing is out of the question. They like the notion of hand washing, however. Three basins are prepared for the washing. First: Pilate's Basin. Warm scented water and blood red hand towels. What they hear is: "Remember, you cannot wash away your sins." Second:

The Basin of Baptism. Warm water in the baptismal font and white linen napkins. Members of the confirmation class remind us all: "Remember your baptism and be thankful." The Servant's Basin is last. Enamel dish pan from the church kitchen, cold water, and dish towels. "Do this in memory of me." They come to the communion table and stretch out their well-washed hands for the gifts of God for the people of God.

GOOD FRIDAY

The ugly gray cross that has been stored in the attic for God knows how long is up, right beside the altar, draped in black. Christmas candles stripped of their red bows are gradually extinguished in the sanctuary windows. A young man, recently released from jail, reads the gospel. The Old Ladies Class removes every sign of color and life from the chancel. There is a long sigh as the last light, the Christ candle, is carried down the aisle and out.

HOLY SATURDAY

I conduct a committal service. I'm distracted as I walk away from the grave, brushing the dirt and snow from my hands. It's been such a hard, cold year. The late snow, the number of deaths and layoffs, the graying of the leaders, and the leaving of the young will make Easter preaching harder than I think I can manage.

I wanted to fill the church with the sight and smell of new life. The shrinking number of orders for lilies for the sanctuary measures the sense of this community's demise. One look at the cost of a single plant had deep-sixed the idea that I could fix it for them.

I stop at the hearse to say good-bye to the wife of the man I've helped to bury. The widow's from out of town, not a member of this church, but no one else is available for her husband's last need. The funeral director, she, and I are the only ones in a country graveyard on this cold Holy Saturday. I hold her hands, tell her again that this is part of my ministry, and ask her to join us for Easter if she's still in town tomorrow. We turn to look at his gravesite. The ground is white with snow; so is the gravesite. It's covered with dozens and dozens of lilies. I can't help my start of surprise.

When she asks me for the third time what she can do to thank me, I tell her. Would she be willing to share those lilies, take the signs of loss and let them witness to a love that was stronger than death? Without another word she walks back to the grave and begins to gather the lilies. The director and I offer to help. Her hands are badly crippled. She declines, smiling. "He would love this. Let me."

EASTER

The congregation gathers. The cross is still covered in black. They're restless, thinking I've forgotten in the sunrise service rush. As we begin the first hymn, "Christ the Lord is risen today" the ushers take the drape down. The sight and scent fills the sanctuary. Every gray, ugly inch of the cross is covered with lilies. In darkness it begins. In light it is finished. Ashes to ashes. Easter to Easter. Christ is risen.

> The religion of the churches and the organized faiths re-
> mains, for better or for worse, the dominant form that reli-
> gion takes today and the permanent depository of the most
> ancient religious narrative. They provide religion with a crit-
> ical mass, with a structure and social constancy without
> which it would likely disappear or dissipate. They provide
> permanent structures—buildings and institutions and com-
> munities—within which the great narratives are preserved,
> interpreted, and passed on to the next generation.[3]

Here is stuff that helps ground our daily life in holy human time. These are the ways we learn to tell time in ways that defy oblivion. The embedded narratives from scripture are interwoven with the limited, heterogeneous repertoire of inherited bits and pieces of our lives. The immense appeal of narrative can be documented in books, ad campaigns for stock brokers, credit cards, members of Congress, cereal boxes, and cell phones. A story sells stuff. Things are used to market time. Witness the enduring popularity of "telling time" through the holy days of Hallmark. We need to lay hands on this stuff and use it to resist being turned into nothing more than commodities. We need to remember how to repair time itself.

Valentine's Day

The last thing I need in a valentine
is some underclad cupid
aiming to puncture an overworked will
and my last reserves of control.
Unbuttoned hope just leads to exposure.
Any extremity of emotion
brought on by Hallmark
deserves all the frostbite it finds.

Life's temperature gauge
Has been down so long,
zero is up.
No plaster saint can convince me
there's a point to hearts and flowers.
Even chocolate loses its appeal,
when you pack it in your pocket,
and get stuck in a snowdrift for days.

When the threat of brimstone
begins to make sense
and headlines the news,
it's time to rekindle Pentecost's fire.
Didn't he say
"Keep the peace and pass the salt"?
Or was it
"Hold your salt and pass the peace"?

Didn't he promise
the Spirit would find us
stranded on ice,
stiff as a board,
frozen with fear and snow-blind?

Check the calendar.
When can we turn up the heat?
Isn't this the season
our ears should start to tingle
and our hearts get strangely warm?[4]

What do the stories of Jesus and the community of the Risen One require and provide? Time to catch our breath. Time to learn to tell time in light of the incarnation. Being willing to risk making contact with the irreducible diversity of the stories of humans who are created imago dei. We need to learn to let these narratives get under our skin and get our nerves working again. It requires an openness to the unfinishedness of creation that's difficult to sustain in face of the addictive rhetoric of the marketplace where time is more than money—it's blood. And speaking of blood, some historians of human festivals trace Valentine's Day to an ancient Roman ritual called Lupercalia, which was thought to ensure protection from wolves.

Trust ancient Romans to know
it takes heart,
fire,
and the color of blood
to keep the wolf away from the door.[5]

Our experience of loneliness, and our attempts to keep the wolf away from the door can be told within a community, and in the telling some of the fractures between lived time and cosmic time can be bound together. Link a story to a thing and the sheer materiality of story-forming stuff will help to bind our minds together. *Homo reparans*, the human impulse to repair things as well as relationships, is a powerful tool in making community.

The Broken Chalice

WHAT HAPPENS WHEN STORIES COLLIDE or when life discrepancies threaten foundational meaning? We experience a spatio-temporal dislocation and begin to search for the lost sense of integrity. Competing narratives can sometimes be resolved by integration. One story may widen to accommodate an alternative narrative within itself. Two worldviews form an organic partnership. Some narrative forms resist integration and appear to demand the suppression or extinction of a competing worldview. I don't know how this story ends — organic partnership or extinction of a competing worldview? Others involved in this narration may dispute this version, this interpretation of a broken cup. I only claim that this is what I have seen and truly believe.

Tuesday morning, May 5, 2004, the General Conference of the United Methodist Church has just completed its morning session. The announcements are read. Grace is said, and the body is dismissed for lunch or for the daily service of Holy Communion. It's not been business as usual. Some delegates are openly weeping, some confidently smiling at the votes that held the line, some shaking their heads, weary of the struggle over homosexuality that has become the code word for church division. Those in the side bleachers stand silently, wearing rainbow-colored stoles and holding out signs with photos of a young man or woman that they're wearing like talismans over their hearts: "My child is of sacred worth."

The church has spoken. Delegates have voted to make more explicit the church's position that "homosexuality is incompatible with

Christian teaching," although a clause is added that United Methodists "will seek to live in Christian community."[8] Ordination remains closed to those who believe themselves to be called by Christ if they are self-avowed, practicing homosexuals. Attempts to strengthen the language that protects equal rights regardless of sexual orientation is defeated. By the time the conference is over, the list of chargeable offenses has been lengthened as well as strengthened. "Those offenses include not being celibate in singleness or being un-faithful in a heterosexual marriage; being a self-avowed practicing homosexual; and conducting ceremonies that celebrate homosexual unions or performing same-sex wedding ceremonies.[9] War-monger-ing, hate crimes, and racism don't make the list this year.

"Open hearts. Open doors. Open minds." It's a church's advertis-ing slogan that is becoming a judgment call. Today it's more accurate to speak of broken hearts and of closing doors for those who had hoped that baptism would be reclaimed as a sacrament of equality.

Those of us who remain in the hall are invited to the table that is being prepared for celebration of the sacrament. The numbers of del-egates and visitors who remain for this lunchtime devotion have steadily grown each day. We cluster around the raised platforms where the table is set with the chalices, the bread, candles, and linen.

There is some singing, but it doesn't cover the sound of weep-ing, at least where I'm standing. The service begins; the words of the liturgy vibrate in the air. Words that hurt but were intended to heal. "By your Spirit make us one with Christ, one with each other . . ." I stretch out my hands to receive the bread and hear a question in my head, "What father, when his child asks for bread, gives the child a stone?" (Matt.7:9). I hold it, waiting for the cup of forgive-ness to come. An older version of the invitation to the table is stirred up like restless heartburn. ". . . and are in love and charity with your neighbors . . ."[10]

I don't feel that I'm in love and I can't even count on charitable feelings about some of my neighbors, at least not right now, not today. I'm probably not fit for the communion table. I turn to go, un-sure what to do with the bread. A sacramental dilemma. I eat it as I walk away; the bread tastes salty. My fingers are coated with the residue of tears.

Over the singing there's a sudden sound of shattering. I'm too far away; I turn back but I can't see how or who or what's been broken. The sound of shock keeps echoing, growing. A clay chalice lies shattered. Someone has deliberately broken a cup of forgiveness. A bishop is on his knees picking up the pieces. Others kneel to help. I head for the exit, and find a cup of coffee. My hands are cold; I need warming.

The session resumes its business. We have a foot of paper to turn into mission before the day is over. I can't keep my place on the page. There are two super screens hanging to the left and right of the assembly, and at the center of both is a projection of a large votive candle and the broken pieces of a chalice wrapped in white linen.

I can't look away from the brokenness. I find myself hoping for floor debate, bishops' rulings, anything to turn the camera's eye away from what's lying on the white linen. I sense the emerging form of the terrible story that this thing is beginning to tell. These shards will be our reality. We will be broken, no longer united. The last time we divided as a church was over slavery, a foreshadowing of a nation divided in civil war. I ask a reserve to take my seat on the floor. I need to get some breathing room. A prophetic shattering straight out of the book of Jeremiah. A sacramental violation that breaks a body of Christ to pieces. If I'd only seen what actually happened, the conflicting truth claims might resolve themselves.

I begin asking about what I missed. An ordained elder broke the cup deliberately. Some say he snatched it out of the bishop's hand and hurled it, throwing the juice on those around him. Some tell me he carefully emptied the cup, lifted it, paused and then dropped it. They are the ones who said he'd been crying. I don't know who he is, or what he looks like, but I do know someone else has been crying. Barbara Day Miller, the conference worship leader, a gifted musician, ordained deacon, and assistant dean of worship at a seminary. It was her personal chalice, sent by the Order of Deacons to be used at General Conference as a gift to celebrate her ordination. Out of all those identical chalices without a history or a story, hers was different. It was the one chosen. Hers was the one broken.

I watch her lead us in singing throughout the afternoon. The broken edges get sharper with each layer of knowing. There's a long history of struggle between the ministers of music and the ministers of word and sacrament. We teach classes about how to handle the conflict of gifts and graces and guaranteed salaries and medical benefits. The privilege and burden of serving tables was part of the original work of a deacon; but those were the days when holy dining was also human dining. Real food. Real tables. Now we use only bread (sometimes real) and juice, and deacons are limited to assisting an elder.

The brokenness makes headlines. The picture of Bishop Ott picking up the pieces, assisted by those wearing rainbow stoles, is featured. For some, the incident is now an example of why unity is impossible with violent people who willfully violate the sacraments. For others, this breaking was a prophetic sign that we had failed to recognize the work of the Spirit. Some conservative leaders are talking openly about irreconcilable differences. An unauthorized proposal for separation is directly released to the media before it is introduced as a resolution. Local congregations watching the news suddenly know more than we do about a house dividing. Even without due process, we're discussing divorce in the hallways.

A group of delegates begin work on a resolution on unity. We're still looking at broken pieces, however. I tell myself that it's not my responsibility. I've not been appointed *homo reparans* for this conference. I go up to touch the pieces during a break. I wonder how I could get them off the table. The afternoon is a time of holy human conferencing. We vote, we argue, we sing, we pray. We listen to our diversity and the growing question of unity. I talk to the young woman behind the camera during the next break. She shares my sense that something needs to be done. Seeing is believing.

I go to Barbara first. I ask her if I may have the pieces. I don't know what may come of my request. But I need to ask her permission to try and repair or at least release the pieces from their captivity. She hugs me hard. This has been a violation of her body and spirit. I pray whatever comes next offers her some form of consolation.

I ask Bishop Ott for the pieces. Would he be willing to hand them to me at the close of communion today? I can't simply take them. They belong to the body. I ask him to tell the community that gathers at the table that there's an open invitation to join me in the lobby. We're going to work at restoration, by whatever means we're given, but time is running out.

The bishop keeps his promise, as I expected. What I didn't expect was the holy mystery that suddenly opens in front of me like a chasm. He wraps the broken pieces so tenderly, so sadly together in the linen cloth. I suddenly know what this really is. He walks towards me holding the broken chalice like the broken body of Jesus. I fall into the chasm of the holy otherness of God, knocked off balance by beauty and terror.

I'm left holding the linen-wrapped thing. I need help getting up. Several people surround me with offers to help. I ask them to come to the lobby. I've prepared a table, located a first aid kit with bandages. The camera woman had located some kind of glue. Some one stops and asks me if I want to invite the man who broke the chalice. They'll take a note to him if I want to write it. I'm still a little off balance. I give someone the cloth and write a note to someone I've never met, asking if he wants to help try to recover some unity in our brokenness.

The group that gathers in the lobby is a mix of laity and clergy, strangers to each other, mainly women. The single man is a delegate from Russia; he speaks no English, but he immediately sets to work on sorting the pieces. Over the hour, some hard facts emerge. Too many pieces are missing. The shattering was complete. The upper bowl won't hold together. We are impatient with the glue. We don't have time to wait to see if it will hold. Is there enough to bring anything new out of the old before the closing communion?

The base gradually emerges from four separate chunks, with hairline fractures. They start to cohere. A man has been watching us work, standing at a distance. He moves almost reluctantly closer and asks, "Can I join you?" "Yes," I say, not taking my eyes off the two pieces I'm coaxing to stay together, "anyone is welcome." "You invited me." Now I look up. "You need to know that I'm the one who broke it. I'm James Preston."

"Everyone is welcome here. You're welcome here." He pulls up a chair and sits down. I hand him the pieces of the cup and go to look for a photographer. I don't know anything about him, but I know from experience that he may need protection. I want a picture of him, of all of us trying to repair more than a broken cup.

Whatever we do, we must do quickly. The final communion service is fast approaching. There's too much brokenness; too many pieces are missing. The chalice needs to be returned to the table, but for what purpose? Paul Ricoeur may be right; there's something unrepairable about human life. The young camera woman, Deborah, is an artist of *bricolage*, however. She pulls jewelry wire out of her purse and weaves a silver basket that will hold the pieces of the bowl together.

What do we do to connect bowl to base? What is this chalice good for? One of the women who is obviously good at repairing worlds suddenly gets up and walks into the assembly hall. The delegates are taking a break. I hope my delegation understands my obsession with this puzzle, this mystery of clay. She returns with a votive candle. It's the missing piece. We drip wax on the base and then place the votive right in the middle. The sight makes us all hold our breath. The flickering light shines through the empty spaces, makes the silver sparkle and the bandages glow. It fills a need that we didn't know we had, light encountering darkness, and overcoming. This deacon's chalice won't serve as a means of sacrament ever again, but here is holiness indeed. An earthen vessel holding heavenly treasure. We place it carefully on a shelf, waiting until it's time to serve as a means of illumination.

In the end, we are about the business of holy conferencing. We endorse a resolution on unity, by a vote of 869 to 41. The cup is quietly returned to the table along with the others for closing communion. All of them are part of this sacrament, this means of grace.

I stand looking at the cup at the close of the conference, marveling at the healing power of this vessel of clay and silver and first-aid bandages. Bishop Ott joins me at the table and then Barbara comes. We look at the cup in silence, and then he asks, "What will happen to this now?" "It's hers," I say. "It goes where she goes."

"I wish . . . I wish we could take it everywhere, show people, tell them about what it means," he says. He's not taken his eyes off the cup. Barbara points out the truth of the thing. It's too fragile. "Promise me this, then," his voice is very firm. "Promise me, that if our church ever changes its heart and mind about this matter, you will bring this cup back and put it on the table. And if I'm alive, if I'm still alive, I'll preside."

What kind of language is a promise like that? Is it empty or full? Does it bind the future in any way, or is just wishful thinking? Only God knows.

I walk back to my room to pack. I'm heading home to a husband and partner who's feeling a bit abandoned by the months of travel, the paperwork, the calls, the conferencing. I grin when I think about telling him that I figured it out, the reason I was supposed to come. My job was to mend some broken pottery. I've finished with my part in this story.

One year and three months later I'm smiling, more than a little wryly, at my shortsightedness. I may be done, but the cup hasn't finished its part in the holy mystery of Christ's table. It, too, must "hope for what we cannot see." I'm in the balcony with a technician, preparing a PowerPoint projection to be used during the closing communion service at Lake Junaluska. The images are of the chalice. I'm praying that its paradoxical brokenness will lead to healing.

This will be a testing ground for the bishops, elders, leaders who gather on these grounds. The executive director has already passed though a baptism by fire for agreeing to permit this "Hearts on Fire" conference to be held on this historic site of United Methodism. Anyone who attends will probably be accused of promoting homosexuality and "capitulation to lifestyles that are inconsistent with Christian discipleship.[11]" But making disciples for Jesus Christ is also the primary goal of the Reconciling Ministries Network, "a national grassroots organization that exists to enable full participation of people of all sexual orientations and gender identities in the life of The United Methodist Church, both in policy and practice."

This is a theological and political struggle over our understanding of baptism, discipleship, and human sexuality. I've written and rewritten, prayed, planned, and tested every piece of these services. They must be scripturally based, theologically sound, representing the best of our tradition of worship and prayer. The forms of worship must also give room to the freedom of the Holy Spirit.

I have the cup with me, in the form of pictures that tell the story of its origin and rebirth. They will be shown while we pray the prayer of confession. "We have failed to be an obedient church. We have not done your will, we have broken your law."[12] James, the breaker and mender of the cup, will be preaching. I plan to show him the pictures. What he preaches may or may not involve the cup, but the Spirit has quietly insisted that I not leave it behind. Somehow, some way, it will be needed.

I expect the carefully generated letter campaign from the Good News leadership and the UMAction, which is linked to the Institute on Religion and Democracy. They want this conference barred from the grounds or boycotted if we're allowed to gather. Their calls for support elicit a surprising volunteer force, the presence of the Ku Klux Klan, which then brings the FBI and local law enforcement agencies to a conference entitled, "Hearts on Fire."

It is a week of Pentecostal fire and holy conferencing, even though, and possibly because, we are ringed with daily reminders of the precious right of freedom of worship. We open our first service with an offering to the United Methodist Committee on Relief (UMCOR) for those who are suffering from Hurricane Katrina. The basins for our renewal of baptism are used first to gather more than fifteen thousand dollars. Then we move to the salty tears of suffering, and our basins of baptism hold the waters of death and new life in Christ.

I've left a piece unfinished that I work at completing throughout the conference. Normally a bishop presides at a communion service. There will be seven in attendance, but they're here to listen, learn, and lead a panel discussion. If this is going to be as controversial as I suspect, should I even ask? No bishops, then, but one who might have been. I finally arrive at the name, Vicki Woods, a well-seasoned leader with a New Englander's sense of spine. She was a leading candidate for bishop but was undermined by the backlash to her public witness among others that led to an arrest on charges of disturbing the peace at the last General Conference. It seemed to me that she's earned the right to be at the table where Christ invites all, all to come and receive the bread of life and share in the cup of blessing.

I tell James that I finally have a presider for the service where he's preaching. "You don't know, do you?" is his response. I apparently don't. "Vicki's the one who prayed with me during communion. She's the one who confirmed that I needed to do what I was afraid of doing. She promised to walk with me up to the table and stand along-side me so I wouldn't have to be alone."

I don't know, but I'm not surprised. I just need to hold on and pay attention to whatever comes next. We gather at the table to sing, praise, pray, and receive the Word of life. There's such a deep silence when the images of the cup are shown that I think people have stopped breathing. James stands and begins to preach up a holy human storm. Elishah's fiery heart burns at the center of his text. Some of the missing pieces of the cup story are restored. He would have settled for crumbs, he said. Just crumbs. Some word of recognition of the broken hopes and hearts, some word of consola-tion for the bolted doors, some word of hope. No crumbs were of-fered. His former bishop served him without a word. Any acknowl-edgment of the hurt would have been enough. One word, one crumb for a broken body. But nothing was said, so a cup was lifted and broken.

He offers those at this table in Junaluska a word of brokenness, but also a word of hope. He calls us to the place in the future where there will be more than crumbs for those who love Christ.

Mark Miller's music comes straight out of the sermon like a whirlwind of song. The image of the broken chalice appears on the screen if by magic. People begin to dance in the aisle. I'm helping to prepare the table, so I miss seeing the woman who leaves her seat and makes her way up on the stage. She hands something to James. The song is finished. The table is ready. I sit down beside him as the Great Thanksgiving begins. He presses something into my hand. It's a piece of broken pottery. He whispers, "She said she knew that she was sup-posed to bring it to Junaluska." I get up, wordless, and place it on the table, beside the cups as the people recite, "Christ has died. Christ is risen. Christ will come again." When the time comes to pronounce the blessing, I simply hold it up and promise, "Some day, some day soon. The brokenness will pass away. Peace is on its way." We hope for what we can not see.

A missing piece brought to the table by a mother whose son, Jonah, picked it up from the floor at General Conference. *Homo reparans.* After the service I tell her that I can't keep the piece. The cup isn't finished. The story isn't over. I ask her to take it home to Jonah and ask him to keep it safe for all of us until he receives the sign. She smiles, very teary, and says that I'm asking a lot of the mother of a seventeen-year-old. I tell her that any mother who has the audacity to name her son Jonah surely knows what she's doing. She'll be fine.

five   EVIDENCE OF THINGS NOT SEEN

The final pieces of this collection address themselves to the nature of hope and human time as described in Romans 8:25. "We hope for what we do not see." These are open-ended narratives that require a frame of reference beyond the here and now. Time can be made human and holy in and through its telling. Here is how we re-collect who we are and who we might become. Proust reminds us that the necessarily true book in each of us is in the form of a story. We are creatures many stories high, stuffed with the recollection of things past that help us to regain the present and imagine the future.

> In describing objects one can make those things which figure in a particular place succeed one another indefinitely; the writer takes two different objects, posits their relationship and encloses it within the circle of "style."[1]

These are the stories of things that help us hope while waiting to see. And while we're waiting for the broken circle to be mended, we remember to plant trees, wait on tables, sing songs, and tell stories about those people and things we've loved, lost, and hope to find again. Above all we must expect to be surprised.

A Broken Shell

A SHELL IS ONE OF THE OLDEST SYMBOLS of baptism in both Judaism and Christianity. It's inscribed in the clay of the catacombs in Rome and painted on the walls of a fourth-century synagogue in Dura-Europos. Baptismal fonts bear the sign of the shell, and sometimes in Lent a congregation is invited to pass by a baptismal basin that holds water and small shells and select one as a reminder of each person's baptism.

We hold a large shell to our ear and we're drawn into childhood's mystery of a sea we can hear but not see. I have a shell that sings of absence and presence. It's old, in terms of human years of habitation. It was a gift from a widow whose house was a marvel and a terror of trash and treasure. She was in her nineties and didn't part with any thing easily, but she pushed the shell into my hands. Her uncle brought it to her when she was eight years old. She couldn't remember which ocean it was from or how it got broken. I used it for baptisms when I wanted to remember the communion of saints.

Every time I lift it and listen these days, the shell reminds me of Kevin, a sea-loving music-making boy, part of our family tree. He lost his life on the edge of the ocean, trying to save a friend. I know how a shell works; no mystery, just an echo of our own being. We hear an echo of ourselves, yet there is mystery. We are buried with Christ in our baptism; we are drawn from killing waters and raised to new life. This shell and one who died young teach us to listen to every heartbeat as if it were a song.

FOR A SURFER WHO RIDES DEEP SLEEP LIKE A WAVE

Raised among mountains,
I'm wary of the sea.
Down to earth,
well, I hope, grounded,
I prefer the rock of ages to the ingrained shifty sand.

Why, then, at the ebb tide of sleep,
does your son appear on my horizon,
surfing with the dolphins,
sporting strands of pearls?

He's far too distant for proper introduction,
but I recognize his frame,
and he seems to wave a greeting
as he crests the final deep
calling Leviathan's name.

Sometimes in sober light
I study his profile and wonder,
"Who can interpret this dream?"
But casual/causal conversation about the deep of grief
is like setting to sea in a sieve,
so I scribble a note, bottle the dream, toss it into the mail.
I trust that it's buoyed to your shore.

I miss your seaward son.
I listen for him in the sound of the shell
I keep on my shelf apart from dust or duty.
Does he laugh?
Heartfelt and fine.
Does he sing?
Sweet. So sweet and low.
I catch a tune in the undertow.
I've a gift from the sea that carries your name.
I thought you'd like to know.[2]

Harvesting Hope

WHAT DO WE DO while we're waiting for what we hope to see? Plant trees. From Kenya to Kentucky, this is a holy human action that roots us in the present and branches out to a future only God can see.

The following litany was developed to be used as part of an entire worship service, but it can also be used as a ritual on its own. Invite children to carry in baskets of apples at the beginning, and lead the group in singing the Appleseed Grace. They can distribute the apples at the conclusion of the litany or give the apples as people come forward to receive communion. The readers can either read the stories or someone can narrate them as storytellers.

LEADER: A sower went out to sow.
Sing the appleseed song: "O, the Lord is good to me."

PEOPLE: **Keep us as the apple of your eye.**
Hide us in the shadow of your wings.

LEADER: You can count the seeds in an apple,

PEOPLE: **but who can count the apples in a seed?**

READER 1: The apple is a fruit of the tree *pyrus malus.* Usually grown in temperate regions, it was introduced to America from England in 1629. It's become a classic image of excellence in education and "A is for apple" has been posted in countless classrooms in this country for almost two centuries. An apple for a teacher was once a way for a student to say "Thank you," but apple-polishing is still not advised by one's peers, unless of course you're talking about iPods or computers.

The connection between eyes and apples and pupils is also a traditional one. Hear the words of the psalmist: "Keep me as the apple of your eye . . ." (Psa. 17:8). In the nineteenth century "apple of your eye" also meant "pupil." The pupil of one's eye was named from the Latin word *pupilla*. When Romans looked into someone's eyes they saw a tiny reflection of themselves, like a child, so seeing one's self was always a learning experience. To see eye to eye is to see as we are seen, the Apostle Paul writes. We are made in the image of God, and we are seen as the pupil, in the apple of God's eye.

Traditionally scholars have translated the fruit of "the knowledge of good and evil" as an apple. Biblical botanists think the fruit was probably a pomegranate, an apricot, or a fig. Who connected apples and snakes? Hard to tell, but in medieval days, red was the mythological color for sexuality.

I earned an A in apple theology my second year in seminary, but the lesson itself was learned down on the farm. Reading week in institutions of higher education is still geared to a largely forgotten agricultural calendar, but it gave me the excuse to head for the hills of West Virginia. I arrived in time to help with picking, pealing, canning, and freezing apples. The old apple tree beside the farmhouse had survived a fiery trial when the house was destroyed. Its apples weren't large, but made good pies. It was the stuff of legend; claims to kinship with Johnny Appleseed were part of the mythmaking mischief of my grandfather. The orchard by the barn had been planted in honor of my parents' twenty-fifth anniversary, but the fruit produced fed more deer than humans.

I pulled up a chair beside Grandma's rocker that was in the shade and we peeled and sliced through most of the morning. I regaled her with stories of my misfit days at a southern bastion of righteousness. She mainly listened. I seem to have gotten the talkative genes from my grandfather's side. In the middle of a long pause, she suddenly said, "It wasn't an apple." It didn't exactly make sense even though we were surrounded with apples, but you can say whatever whenever it strikes your fancy if you're past ninety.

Since I'd been telling stories about my Old Testament class, perhaps what she's doing is exegesis, scripture interpretation. "You mean, it wasn't an apple in the Garden of Eden?" "Right. It wasn't an apple."

It wasn't, at least according to scriptural sources, but I had to go to seminary to learn that it was probably a fig, or a pomegranate. How did she arrive at her conviction?

"Why wasn't it an apple?" "Because you can trust an apple." That's certainly a bottom line. God, Mother, and apple pie suddenly has a context. My curiosity gets stronger than a sense of discretion. What did she think it was, since it couldn't be an apple?

"A banana," she said with a perfectly straight face. I managed to put my paring knife down before I collapsed in hysterical laughter. Visions of Mae West and the Marx Brothers cavorting in the orchard! I finally catch my breath when she bushwhacks me again. "How else do you explain the fall of man?"

LEADER: You can count the seeds in an apple,

PEOPLE: but who can count the apples in a seed?

READER 2: "An apple a day keeps the doctor away." This folk wisdom contains some of the apple's attributes as a healthy food. Apples lack fat, sodium, and cholesterol. They're packed with nutrients such as thiamine, riboflavin, and phosphorous. They are now known to be fortified with quercetin, a flavonoid that may help prevent cancers of the lungs, skin, and colon. Fiber. Iron. Natural sweeteners. Calcium. But in case you need a little sugar you can have: apple betty, apple butter, apple cider, apple cobbler, apple crisp, apple cake, apple compote, apple dumplings, apple fritters, apple jack, apple juice, apple pie, apple pudding, and apple preserves. You can medicate yourself with baked, bleached, cooked, crab-, dried, fried, candied, caramel, stewed, or plain fresh apples. Just what the doctor ordered.

A sower went out to sow. Farming's tough. Being land-based in a culture that commutes for a living is tough. Being rooted in an uprooted time is tough. Being an industry that regularly suffers from "acts of God"—what with tornados, droughts, frost, floods, and mortgages—that is not only rough, and tough, but also really addictive. It's something that people with clean fingernails never understand.

So what's the good news in this story about seeds? That it's all good seed. The trustworthiness of God is underlined in that one small fact: all the seed is good, capable for bringing a new creation to light and life. There are no bad seeds in this story.

A sower went out to sow . . .

But folks who farm might ask a question about God's intentions when they get to the rocky soil. God should have known better? You don't normally sow wild oats or hybrid corn in some stranger's field. You sow what you know, your own ground. So why did the sower throw good seed on hard ground? Hope is easily sprouted, but hard to harvest. Why risk the very source of your survival? Why throw good seed on stone-hard ground?

I asked an old farmer (called Grandpa Cabbagehead, for reasons I never understood) why the sower threw perfectly good seed on stony soil. He asked me a question as a way of answering. "How long do you plan to be farming?" "That," he said, "is the right question to ask."

A seed encounters a rock. Spouts roots, creeps into cracks, struggles for room, dies. What happens to the rock? One very small piece is cracked open. It's the first step in a rock becoming soil. That sower was sowing for the future that may be a long time coming, but she was making room for a harvest that someone will see.

READER 3: Apples don't normally escape from orchards and grow in the wild. An unexpected presence can usually be explained by the bees, except of course, for the ones planted by the real life legend named John Chapman but known as Johnny Appleseed.

Apples require several years to reach bearing age. Very fruitful trees are slower to come into fruit than trees that bear normally. Prepare the soil in fall for a spring planting. For fertilizing good news, see Luke 13:6–9. Aged manure is advised. If you want to prune an apple tree you need to prune when you first plant it and then repeat yearly. Thin out weak and tangled branches to let sunlight into the center. You'll need to go easy on the old-timers if they haven't been tended to in some time. Don't try to force an old tree into a new shape, but you can prune it along the lines it's been growing into over the years.

READER 4: If you ever wonder if the Creator likes variety, make a list of apples: Akane, Ben Davis, Cortland, Dolgo Crab, Empire, Golden Delicious, Granny Smith, Gravenstein, Grimes Golden, Jonagold, Liberty, Limbertwig, Macoun, McIntosh, Newtown

Pippin, Northern Spy, Red Delicious, Rome Beauty, Shockley, Spartan, Stayman, Winesap, and last, but not least, the Yellow Delicious, courtesy of West by God Virginia and Johnny Appleseed.

> The stories of God require those who know the stories by heart. A congregation, like a child, asks that we not only read a story, but tell a story. Here, the word is not just talk; drink the cup with this community and hear what the cup says of God and the hope for God's world. Here, "Jesus" is not just a name from the past, capable of being used for whatever purpose the speaker chooses; this bread given to you is who he is."[3]

Lip Service

WHAT DO YOU LAY YOUR HANDS ON when time is running out? What do you reach for when you want to entrust your greatest treasure to your child?

In the early church, *traditio* was the handing on of tradition, a creed that held the codes of life and faith. It was the responsibility of every member of the community of Christ, the Beloved of God, to participate in *traditio*. You can still see evidence of this when Bibles are given to young children, and then again when they graduate or enter the military. A grandson reads words from his grandmother's Bible at her service of death and resurrection and you hear and see the handing on of holy things.

I have a Bible I've been saving for our son. It was given to me by Judy Craig, one of the brave-hearted band of United Methodist women who sit in the bishop chairs. I'd been invited to be the preacher for her conference. The wisdom tradition in scripture was being studied in imaginative ways. I was packing for what promised to be a controversial conference. The theological firestorm over Sophia was in full force, then the backlash blew in our front door. Our son attempted to take his life.

Somewhere between the tears, terror, anger, doctors, lawyers, and police, I remembered to call her to cancel. Daniel heard me on the phone and asked me not to. It would make him feel worse. The thought of preaching made me feel a whole lot worse than worse. He asked me to go, to keep the promise I'd made. I made my excuses to whoever was holding on the other end of the line and told them I'd be there.

I was, just barely. Bill had had to pry me out of the truck at the airport; every maternal instinct was up in arms. I forgot to pack my toothbrush, my Bible, and most of my sense of humor. The bishop made arrangements to supply all the missing articles. My battered sense of humor was restored when I realized that she'd assigned two superintendents as body guards since some of the conference members were picketing in protest over having a redheaded heretic as their preacher.

I keep the Bible that she gave me as evidence of things hoped for, not seen. She sent it as a gift to Daniel, but he isn't inclined to lay hands on something being used as a weapon. I remind him every so often that he might want to read the book with his name on it, but he thinks church is a big disappointment to Jesus. Just lip service, he says. Hymns are the only form of music he avoids once he leaves home.

This Bible sits on a variety of shelves over the next ten years. I use it only when I can't find the annotated version when planning a worship service. I like to keep it close by, however, particularly during Holy Week. Maybe this is the season when all those psalms Daniel sang as a choir boy begin their mysterious work in his bloodstream. Maybe this is the night when he'll hear all that is holy call him by name.

What we hear on Wednesday, Holy Week, is a cry for help. He's trying not to let his anxiety flood the phone line, but all the red lights go on. He's been mugged, but not to worry, it's just his face that took a beating. Some homeless guy asked him for money as he locked up after work and walked to his car, but he didn't have a dime. We believe him. He lives on tips and minimum wage in order to make music and market new bands with his older cousin Ian in the city of the angels.

Maybe it would have made a difference. Maybe not. He takes several punches then pushes back hard, and makes it to the car and then home. That was Monday night, this is Wednesday, and there's something wrong. He's been to the emergency room twice, but his fever keeps building and something is wrong with his mouth. Should we come? No, it's Holy Week. He just wants us to know, and you know, pray for him. Ian will keep us posted because Daniel's having trouble talking.

Bill keeps him on the phone while I begin to check out tickets online. I'm heading west by dawn the next day while Bill tries to prepare for Maundy Thursday services. A Last Supper is the last thing he wants to be leading. Ian is a lifeline, keeping us posted, making sure Daniel's not alone. He's been put in intensive care, his mouth infected from a cut with a virulent strain of staph. The antibiotics don't seem to be having any effect.

What do you lay your hands on when time is running out? What do you reach for when you want to ensure your child's survival? We pack music CDs, family pictures, his stuffed lion, and on top of everything, a wine colored Bible that has been waiting on a shelf.

Traditio. I want to hand him life, but that's out of my reach. I want to give him faith, but that's not a human to human exchange. Hope, then. Can I bring him hope? Play him songs that he loves? But what happens if he won't sing again?

I open his Bible to the place where I find the voices that console, call, and terrify me, all in the book called Isaiah. Here is a priestly singer of holy altars and angels; here is the one who sings the songs of the Suffering Servant; here is the one who posts the watchers on a ruined city's walls and teaches them to keep God and the people awake by keeping a noisy watch through the night.

I know what I've got in my hands. I don't know if I can bear to hand it to him. I carry the book like a bomb past the airport security, into a taxi, and then though the hospital corridors. I have to put it down so that I can be gloved, masked, and tied into a uniform. I'm not supposed to touch him. I'm not supposed to take anything into his room. The head nurse and I square off about the Bible. It may have to be burned if I take it in. I tell her she can burn it after he gets well, but not until then.

The news is that they've identified what's infected him. The mugger was probably dumpster diving in medical waste. The good news is that a new antibiotic hit the market four months ago and it's had good results. The best news would be that it's going to save his lower lip and his life.

I don't want to try to find words for what I learned about love and fear when I walked into his room. It is enough to remember how my hands shook and my voice wavered as I tried to hand him the most powerful medicine that I know. I opened his Bible and read:

And I said, "Woe is me! I am lost, for I am a man of unclean lips, and I live among a people of unclean lips; yet my eyes have seen the King, the LORD of hosts!"

Then one of the seraphs flew to me, holding a live coal that had been taken from the altar with a pair of tongs. The seraph touched my mouth with it and said: "Now that this has touched your lips, your guilt has departed and your sin is blotted out."

Then I heard the voice of the Lord saying, "Whom shall I send, and who will go for us?" And I said, "Here am I; send me!" (Isa. 6:5–8)

When the medicine finally kicks in, his fever begins to drop and the infection starts to recede. He asks Ian and me to help him type up the words to the songs that they've recorded. Just in case. They may have to remove part of his lip. Each day he gets a little better. And he's finally told he'll be released from the hospital with lip and life still in one piece. We're both scorched around the edges. As I pack up my bag in his room, I wipe the wine-colored leather book and its edges with the gel that protects us from 97 percent of our tiniest of foes and sneak it out with my things.

I pack to return east. I'm not taking the Bible. I can risk being a nagging mama now. I hand it to him as I leave. It's his. *Traditio.* I suggest that if he really wants to engage the principalities and powers he should read what a truly good protest song should sound like. I tell him it's time to read the book that shares his name.

The week after Pentecost, Bill downloads a song from Daniel that's posted on his website. We sit in the pastor's study and listen to our son sing something that sounds completely different yet familiar. I think it's what happens when the psalms and the prophets begin to get into your bloodstream. It's something to hope for.

Go your way, Daniel, for the words are to remain secret and sealed until the time of the end. Many shall be purified, cleansed, and refined . . . But you, go your way, and rest; you shall rise for your reward at the end of the days. (Dan. 12:9–10, 13)

Conversational Music

So I'm back again . . . and you know what that means—
caught by a social contract, undeniably enslaved it seems
that the Master of the Palace has given me a new name,
are we clear?
Don't worry, while this statement might seem strange to
your ear and just a little bizarre
from here on out, for the purpose of Re-Confirmation,
call me CCQ Murray-Bel-te-Shaz'zar
'cause this IS Babylon Working.
So whatever you do
don't do
as they do
and try to deny the visions imparted by a Holy Watcher
concerning divisions of the kingdoms of desert kings.
Check the text.
A spirit of the gods was given graciously,
providing the understanding to interpret these nightmare dreams to
you all
while explaining hermeneutic riddles
when reading the apocalyptic writing on the wall.
Solving problems,
probably not long for this world,
but it doesn't matter,
read between the lines,
I'm a leo signed mad hatter

who only acknowledges one master.
So you gotta be an angel to shut the mouth of this lion
aspiring to bring down those who walk in pride.

Conver-sational music
understands this one thing,
an anthem is just a song
an entire nation can sing

Con-versional music.
Understand this one thing—
a hymn is just a song
all of god's children can sing.

Trapped between truth and the greatest of all lies,
hidden in plane sight, they've no need to disguise
even when they digitally falter,
because the Altar of modern day humanity is Television.
It educates our children while conditioning a mental prison
of an attention span that lasts just long enough for the commercial
break; beats down our natural instincts to the point
as long as we've got reruns of Friends,
who cares what the rest of the world thinks?
The seven deadly sins are in syndication.
So sorry if you're living in an impoverished, brutally governed nation
but we really do care, just ask Sally Struthers, the check's in the mail,
and you can find us in the house of God
every Christmas and Easter without fail.
It's all part of the preplanned package.
Anyone that doesn't live inside our borders
must obviously be a savage and that's the hidden message
        in their add ad.
People are dying without ever getting the chance to enjoy free will
because they've added an asterixed addendum to Thou Shall Not Kill,
you can't impose freedom with force,
but you can definitely assist it,
in fact, I thought that was the reason
the United Nations existed.

Conver-sational music
understands this one thing—
an anthem is just a song
an entire nation can sing.

Con-versional music.
Understand this one thing—
a hymn is just a song
all of god's children can sing.

And this time the message doesn't have to come through
    a burning bush.
You can see with your own eyes that they rush upon us
    like a whirlwind
with humvees and tanks in place of chariots and horsemen.
No one ever expects the Thought Inquisition, but they're a
    vast armada
advancing against countries and passing through them like a flood,
drowning the beautiful land in blood, spreading fear, calling it fact,
tens and thousands will fall victim through cultural ignorance . . .
what do you think about that?
Distracted by democracy deal making,
stretching a long capitalistically clawed arm against the natives,
just like their forefathers did in the days of old,
believing it's their destiny to become the rulers of the treasuries of
black gold and silver raiders.
We didn't lose the Ark . . . it was taken from us for being
    poor caretakers,
but as it is written, the second coming is going to remake us.
Though there shall be a time of anguish such has never occurred since
nations first came into existence.
But when it's past . . . all people shall be delivered at last,
so awaken, members of the heart resistance,
to everlasting life,
where open minded and wise souls shall shine like the brightness
    in the sky,
where no one is an island because the savior is the only survivor

worth watching, and the blessed bind that ties
those who teach righteousness,
will glow like the stars filled with an eternal light that never dies.[4]

> To have a religious sense of life is . . . to tremble with the pos-
> sibility of the impossible . . . that is why religious narratives are
> filled with so many miracle stories, which are stories of trans-
> forming change more stunning than anything Lewis Carroll
> dared imagine could happen to Alice—virgins becoming
> mothers, mountains moving on command, seas parting, the
> dead rising from the grave, and—most importantly, because
> this is what these stories are all about—sinners being forgiven
> and given a new heart, *metanoia*.[5]

The Singer/Storyteller

THE CLERGYWOMEN'S CONFERENCE IN GLORIETTA WAS OVER, but the glow lingered. I'd rented a car so I could roam around in the sunlit Four Corners area before flying back to the hard cold winter of a run-down church in a steel mill town. I think I got high on the sunlight. I know I got lost. Somewhere in New Mexico I saw a trading post and went in to sober up and get directions to the nearest airport. I got one glimpse of the vision as soon as I cleared the door. The bottom shelf. I got on my knees for a closer look. There. What I believed and yet had never seen: the shape and the structure of the soul in search of the Word. There she sat, a storyteller/singer. Her head was thrown back and her mouth formed a perfect O of holy human sound. In her hands she held the seed jar of life, and on it was painted other breathing beings: butterfly, deer. She held the jar and sang and over her shoulders; across her legs the children leaned into the story or song. Their mouths open, they were part of the chorus of life.

I don't know how long I knelt there with my nose against the glass. I could see the price of the vision: four hundred dollars. I didn't dare touch what I couldn't afford. The trader told me the figure came from Second Mesa, a family of women potters. This figure was one by the granddaughter of the first woman who made the first Singer/Teller. He said it was unusual to have a new holy figure emerge so suddenly. The first one appeared in the late '50s, early '60s in the Four Corners region and spread like wildfire.

I got to my feet, thanked him for the story, and left her behind. Physically that is. I carried the vision like a talisman in my mind clear across the country. This is what we do, this is who we are: singers of the songs of the suffering servants, storytellers of the Rising Son. I arrived at our parsonage in West Virginia, still grieving at the absence. Bill met me at the front door with a question. "Guess whose alma mater just called? Duke has invited you to give a lecture called "Images for Worship and Preaching."

I was amazed. I didn't think they even had my address in the alumni files. "Guess how much they're going to pay you?" I knew the answer before he spoke, "four hundred dollars." I spent the next day searching the map to see where I'd become lost so I could find the treasure I'd left behind.

I finally located the trading post, wired the money. They promised to send the Singer/Storyteller first class. I picked up the package on the porch; my delight was drowned in a wave of anxiety. The package rattled.

When I unwrap it, she's in eight pieces. Bill, ever the pragmatic, says, "Send it back. Get another one."

I can't. This one is mine. I've discovered this a little too late. "That can't be the only one," he insists. It isn't, but this one is mine. How can I explain it? I'm going to spend a month's salary on a broken piece of pottery? Can I explain it?

"Look," I show him. "Just look at the child sprawled across her left ankle. He's yawning. I know that look. It happens to me every time I preach. This one is mine."

It takes me a month to piece her back together. The broken Singer/Storyteller, a singer of songs of suffering and hope. Is she a fragile figure of clay, or a mythic figure of immense importance that suddenly emerges from the earth itself? Mere stuff or a force in the universe who holds the jar of life together with a song?

Why would this broken figure be such a potent sign of our times? What else was going on in the Four Corners regions in the '50s and '60s? The atomic testing of matter itself, the splitting of the universe found in an atom. The origin story. The creation of a weapon that can silence all the stories. So what does this broken figure of a storyteller/singer of sacred songs teach us about instruments of peace or the survival of every thing that breathes? I don't know. Something about the possibility of the impossible, I hope.

Why did the world power of Jesus' day conspire against a man who told stories? What was the source of his power, the force of his threat? A handful of nonviolent (more or less), underemployed hill-billies from Galilee? The threat to the empire? I'd say it was his presence and his stories. Jesus told stories that deconstructed the religious and military establishment so thoroughly that these same powers broke their own code of ethics in order to silence him. He took the commonplace things of daily life and constructed a vision of reality that defied convention. A widow's mite, a farmer's seed, a hand towel became the means of hallowing a marginalized community's experience and sustained the memory of God's particular grace for centuries to come.

A Service of Basins and Towels

I wash my hands in innocence, and go around your altar, O LORD, singing aloud a song of thanksgiving, and telling all your wondrous deeds. O LORD, I love the house in which you dwell, and the place where your glory abides. Do not sweep me away with sinners, nor my life with the bloodthirsty, those in whose hands are evil devices, and whose right hands are full of bribes. (Psa. 26:6–10)

These are words of a psalm used by those with sacramental authority for the bread of life. They would pray these words to an ancient song in silence as they prepared to serve the communion table. It's a liturgical gesture that has its origins in simple actions of eating. Wash your hands. The meal is ready. Say grace.

It's a ceremonial custom that should not be carved in stone. "Then the Pharisees and scribes came to Jesus from Jerusalem and said, 'Why do your disciples transgress the tradition of the elders? For they do not wash their hands when they eat'" (Matt. 15:2). What mattered to Jesus was the clean heart; clean hands were often the prerogative of the not-poor.

We sense a need for ritual cleansing, however, in our nation, our neighborhoods, and our selves. Like Pilate, a leading politician in an earlier empire, we've washed our hands of the whole affair one too many times. But this is not the only story we have. We have inherited this story of compulsive washing, as well as a compassionate one where Jesus takes a towel and washes the feet of his friends who will betray him.

The image of Pilate may appear to be intrusive in the traditional Maundy Thursday service of footwashing; it pollutes the concept of being washed. Yet this fused image of hands-water-Pilate-sin can be very powerful if it is incorporated into a service of ritual washing. A "Pilate's basin" is necessary in order to have a servant's basin. These two stories of washings offer paradox and creativity, as the roles of servant and leader are redemptively reversed.

What would a Pilate's basin look like? What kind of towel would be needed? Elegant antiques versus aluminum pitchers, warm-scented water in contrast to cold, wine-colored towels in contrast to church kitchen dishcloths.

But what might move us from "washing our hands of the whole affair" to the cold water of discipleship and the rough edges of dishtowels? A reminder of our baptism.

Three basins, three sets of towels, and three affirmations of faith are the means of moving from washing to being washed to washing again. Pilate's Basin: "Remember, you cannot wash your sins away." The Basin of Baptism: "Remember your baptism and be thankful." The Servant's Basin and the final words before coming to share at the table: "Do this in memory of me."

The first time I held the service was on Maundy Thursday, and the handwashing took place within the communion service. A brief explanation was given before the service began. The passage from the thirteenth chapter of John was the text for the sermon. The eucharistic prayers were offered, and the congregation was invited to the table via the way of the basins. Like the sound of water, the words of each basin mixed and mingled: "Remember, you cannot wash your sins. Remember your baptism and be thankful. Do this in memory . . . Remember . . . Remember . . . Remember . . .

This service has been repeated off and on in various churches for more than twenty years. We need rituals for public/private confession and absolution. We need scripture-shaped things that will help us both confess and receive assurance of pardon. We also need a revitalized awareness of mission, a new understanding of the ministry of the baptized.

The Servant's Basin gains its deepest meaning when those who are the servants of the "servants" stand at a table with a dishpan with cold water that's decorated by the daily newspaper. My most striking memory comes from the service where Sonny, a member with cerebral palsy, wiped our hands with fierce erratic gestures of love. The particular narrative of a community can surface in this service of things. Pilate's basin is often an antique wash basin and pitcher with an origin story attached. The linen napkins often unfolded the unused memories of long-ago weddings or teas. In recent years, I've worked with the symbolism of the dish towels that are used on the third table. For United Methodists, the service of the basins and towels can be linked to Wesley's covenant service.

Christ has many services to be done.
Some are more easy and honorable,
    others are more difficult and disgraceful.
Some are suitable to our inclination and interests,
    others are contrary to both.
In some we may please Christ and please ourselves.
But then there are other works where we cannot please Christ
    except by denying ourselves.
It is necessary, therefore,
    that we consider what it means to be servant of Christ.[6]

The following poem, "Directions for Using a Towel," can be used as part of the sermon or printed in the bulletin as meditation.

DIRECTIONS FOR USING A TOWEL

To be used for:
    Drying dishes.
    Wiping eyes.
    Mopping spilled milk.
    Coping with sighs.
    Cleaning stains.
    Creating scandal.
    Holding on when it's too hot to handle.

    Washing feet.
    Softening jars.
    Binding wounds in a world of scars.

Better than Bounty, thin as skin.
Don't give it up, or throw it in;
It simply grows more holy over time.

For when the one
that death could not defeat
returns, the towel will be a sign
imprinted with *imago Christi* eyes.
All grave and dusty sins are washed away.
God takes us by the hand and helps us rise.[7]

In My Father's House

TELLING TIME IN ALMOST HEAVEN requires more than one timepiece these days. You can find everything from digital to sun dial, and the *Farmer's Almanac* still holds its own once you're outside a city's limits. Folks in small county seats are still waiting for the Verizon man to come calling, but there are signs that even he will be coming round the mountains very soon.

My father returned to this corner of the world when he reached his early fifties because he liked the way they told time in the country. The only warning sign of a midlife crisis came when he asked us if we knew what thirty-five and fifteen amounted to. My sister and I raised our eyebrows at this reminder of our grade school math drills, but answered, "fifty." "Right," he said, "but you won't believe it when it happens to you."

He wanted to grow old in Appalachia because of the shared assumption that you knew a thing or two when you retired. Partly due to the lack of jobs for the young, and partly due to a rural worldviews, there's a common sense of elders having their say in the running of the world. It depends on being able. Able to drive a car, a truck, or a tractor. Able to handle the banking, or the grandbabies. You usher at church, work the bake sale, or help the new preacher repair the furnace. You repair things that are breaking down, keep your tools in good working condition, and that's the sign you're alive and able, a *homo reparans*.

A man and his tools are not easily parted. It took my father both hands to drive a nail when he was eighty-five, but he was counting on being able to drive a nail when he turned ninety. A bleeding ulcer nearly swept him off the ladder of life, but he held on fiercely. I watch him doing arm lifts with Mother's five-pound large print Bible so the doctors will let him go home. Pumping the iron of the gospel gets him home for one more year.

This near brush with finitude sets some internal timepiece working in the family. It's time to deal with the real nitty gritty. Where does he want to be buried? The apple orchard suits him fine. It's the only ground you're able to lay claim to in the long run, he often told us. The only real real estate is your grave.

I call the funeral director, who teaches school as a side hobby. He spends two hours getting the details down. We don't need permission or papers. We can pick a spot, have it dug, and lay a body down. It needs easy access from a road, good drainage, and the choice of container is up to us.

The apple orchard then. It's been left to fend for itself for years. Perhaps we'll plant some young trees and tend to the old ones. He likes the notion and wonders where his pruning tools have gone. We decide to get the orchard ready, avoiding the reasons for our motivation. There aren't many places that let you pick your own ground of being, mixing your own dusty end with the dust of the earth.

We plan to plant a Gala apple and three cherry trees by the barn, and two pear trees facing the road. We couldn't overlook the pears. They're the punch line of his favorite joke: "It wasn't the apple in the tree that caused all the problems; it was the pair on the ground."

It's an old joke at the heart of an old story of a garden, and a fall. It's his story at the end. He stumbles and falls on his way to see a garden. Perhaps there would have been a different ending to this story if we had health care healthy enough to provide for underpaid, overworked practitioners in the healing arts. Whose fault is it? Nurses who forget to put the bedrail up? Orderlies who can't be bothered to read the charts and make him try to walk with a broken back? Doctors who don't notice that he can't breathe? Mother, who feeds him oatmeal delivered by mistake? He chokes and stops breathing. It should end then, but against his will and all the paperwork that says, "Let go," they bring him back from the dead.

By the time I arrive, just back from General Conference, he's tied to a basic tool of life, a ventilator. Now that he's dying, the nursing care in ICU is very good. The nurse is surprised by his response, his eyes clear, his pulse steadies. We sing to him. It's a good thing his hearing aids are off. It's hard to carry a tune at 4:00 A.M. He watches us and seems to be waiting. My youngest sister begins to quietly read to him. My mother wants me to decide about the machines.

When, I wonder, did I agree to be the one who decides about these instruments of life and death? What will happen to my soul, my mind, my own body if I decide to remove these supports for someone who gave me life? What instrumentality of grace is sufficient for this task? A picture of my father comes to mind. He's standing in a field, surrounded by old fence posts. He's been startled by something, and he's laughing. The image of the field stirs up the memory of a gospel song. "Keep your hand on the plow." I know now why you don't look back or turn around. You'll cause pain and confusion if you wobble.

Was he ready to go home? Could he trust Jesus to hold on? He can't answer in words, but I ask him to tell me any way he can. He looks directly at me and slowly blinks both eyes. I asked. I think he just answered. I'll ask him once more after the others have the chance to say good-bye.

The doctors agree that the machines will be turned off; they're being careful to be kind. I go back in. His eyes are steady, focused on my face. I ask again. "Are you ready to let Jesus hold on?" He blinks both eyes again very slowly and looks at me. I nod and touch his forehead, "Jesus, hold on." I tell the nurse that he wants to have the machines removed. The nurse asks us to leave the room so that he can prepare him.

He's clean, free of intrusions, peacefully covered with a blanket tucked carefully around him when we come in again. His eyes are focused above us now. I count the breaths, lighter, lighter. Less and less. We start to sing the "Battle Hymn of the Republic" softly, prompted by what, I don't remember. No breath now. The nurse touches my arm to tell me he's gone. We don't finish the song.

The funeral director comes and removes the body, a worn-out tool that's been laid aside. His ashes will be held in a vase from the Korean War made out of a mortar shell until we get the apple orchard ready. I go back in, just to be sure we've left nothing behind. That's when I notice the carpenter's level resting on the window sill.

I walk over and pick it up, curious that I hadn't seen it earlier. Intensive care rooms ban everything that's not essential to life support. I think about my older sister, who has been his right hand on the farm for most of her life. She probably brought it in to encourage him to get well and come back home. She sat in the hospital for hours, refusing to come in until the very end, looking at pictures of our father working in the field, fixing houses. I carry the level out to where she's waiting in the hallway and offer it to her.

"That's not mine," she says. We look at it together. "I thought you brought it to him, to encourage him. It was in the window by the bed." She shakes her head, silent. A strange notion begins to form, but I'm determined not to let it upset the sensible grip I've got on my soul. I take the carpenter's level back into the ICU and offer it to the male nurse who's cleaning the bed.

"That's not ours," he says. "Are you sure?" I'm very insistent. "It was in the window, right by his bed." He looks it over, and then shakes his head. "It should be marked if it was one of ours."

One last question before I turn loose of the rational. I call the funeral director on his cell phone. It doesn't belong to him. I stare at this object that seemingly materialized into our lives. It's what he tried to do; keep it level and frame it true. *Homo reparans.* An old tune starts dancing in my head.

Ain't gonna' need this old house no longer.
Ain't gonna' need this house no more.
Ain't got time to fix the shingles.
Ain't got time to fix the floor . . .

That's it. I'm not asking again to whom this belongs. I pick up my bag, join the family in the lobby, and walk out of St. Joseph's Hospital with a carpenter's level under my arm.

For Father Joseph

The crèche is on the kitchen table.
I poke through old newsprint and straw
for the well-seasoned saints cloistered
in attics, and stored with old toys.
Mary emerges, serene in her blue.
Baby Jesus is delivered,
a bouncing boy with one lopsided grin
and two ever-loving arms
missing the thumb on each hand.

I arrange the scene in its biblical best;
angels just imagined,
shepherds none too clean.
The wise men remain at a distance,
keeping Epiphany clear.

I brush the dust from Joseph's coat
and note blue lines on his hands.
Stress marks, that's all.
The hint of pain,
the strain in his eyes,
is a trick of the light,
a shadow from the empty stall.

All is calm, all is bright,
still, I'm slow to consign him
to his resigned role:
shaggy as Donkey, contented as Cow.

Once I took his strength for granted.
I should put him in place, but I fear letting go.
No rational reason for holding so tight
except it's the season of apocalyptical readings
and our fathers, our fathers, our fathers
are falling around us, silent like snow.

I feel a draft;
some secret crack in my foundation
lets in a chill.
I sense a need to wrap tight in a creed:
conceived by the Holy Spirit
born of the virgin Mary.

In this Madonna season
I believe in a virgin, complete in herself.
She's too fiercely female to confine to a shelf
or closet too tightly, right out of sight.

But I miss the missing father
on the Christmas stamp this year.
And in the awkward silence
that follows, "Let us pray,"
"Abba?"
"Abba?"
I hear a child say.[8]

notes

INTRODUCTION

1. David Long, *Poets & Writers*, 30/5 (September/October 2002), 23–29.
2. Ibid., 24.
3. Diane Winston, *Red-Hot and Righteous: The Urban Religion of the Salvation Army* (Cambridge and London: Harvard University Press, 1999), 4.
4. Vanessa Ochs, *Miriam's Object Lesson: a Study of Objects Emerging in the New Rituals of Jewish Women* (unpublished thesis, Drew University, 2000), 2.
5. Kathleen Barlow and David Lipset, "Dialogics of Material Culture: Male and Female in Murik Outrigger Canoes" *American Ethnologist* 24/1 (1997), as cited by Ochs, 9.
6. Leonardo Boff, *Sacraments of Life, Life of the Sacraments* (Washington, D.C.: Pastoral Press, 1987), 79.
7. The study of material culture is a scholarly response to these quiddity questions. In this field, some things matter. The recent focus of material culture studies is on how things matter, and to whom and in what ways. The sheer magnitude of materiality, the specificity of specific things prevents a general theory from being easily assembled, but "the theme of object having physical and intellectual consequence" is detailed in Simon Bronner's *Grasping Thing* (Lexington: University Press of Kentucky, 1986).

Chapter One: THINGS THAT SAY GRACE

1. Heather Murray Elkins, originally published as "Acts of God and Other Mysteries" *Weavings*, 21/1 (January/February 2006).
2. Paul Piehler, *The Visionary Landscape*, as cited in John Navone, *Seeking God in Story* (Collegeville, Minn.: Liturgical Press, 1990), 164.

3. Rosemary Radford Ruether and Herman J. Ruether, *The Wrath of Jonah: The Crisis of Religious Nationalism in the Israeli-Palestinian Conflict*, 2nd ed. (Minneapolis: Fortress Press, 2002).

4. James F. White, *Introduction to Christian Worship*, 3rd ed. (Nashville: Abingdon Press, 2000), 201.

5. Heather Murray Elkins © 1987, revised 2005. All rights reserved.

6. Heather Murray Elkins © 1997. All rights reserved.

7. Salman Aktar, MD. *Objects of Our Desire* (New York: Random House, 2005), 67ff.

8. Caroline Walker Bynum, *Holy Feast and Holy Fast: The Religious Significance of Food to Medieval Women* (Berkeley: University of California Press, 1987), 295.

9. Heather Murray Elkins © 2001. All rights reserved.

10. Heather Murray Elkins © Easter 2005. All rights reserved.

11. Heather Murray Elkins © 1989, revised 2001. All rights reserved.

Chapter Two: STORIES AND STRUCTURES OF FORGIVENESS

1. Paul Ricoeur, *Memory, Nativity, Self and the Challenge to Think God*, ed. Maureen Junker-Kenny and Peter Kenny (New Brunswick, N.J.: Transaction Publishers, Rutgers University, 2004), 7.

2. Ricoeur, *Memory*, 10.

3. Ibid.

4. Peter N. Steams, gen. ed., *The Encyclopedia of World History* (Boston: Houghton Mifflin, 2001), 1012–14.

5. Ricoeur, *Memory*, 12.

6. Heather Murray Elkins © 2001. All rights reserved.

7. "The Waiting," Heather Murray Elkins, © 1978. All rights reserved. From *Testimony* (Nashville: Embodied Word Press, 1978), 7.

8. Heather Murray Elkins © 2001. All rights reserved. Words in stanza 6 from Katherine Bates, "America, the Beautiful," 1904.

Chapter 3: THINGS THAT NAME THEMSELVES

1. David D. Hall, ed., *Lived Religion in America: Toward a History of Practice* (Princeton, N.J.: Princeton University Press, 1997).

2. See "Button, Button, Who's Got the Button" in my book *Wising Up: Women, Ritual, and Aging* (Cleveland: Pilgrim Press, 2005), 123–26.

3. Simon Brunner, *Grasping Things* (Lexington: University Press of Kentucky, 1982), 212.

4. Deborah Vansau McCauley, *Appalachian Mountain Religion: A History* (Chicago: University of Illinois, 1995), 16.

5. Northrup Frye, *Anatomy of Criticism* (Princeton, N.J.: Princeton University Press, 1957).

6. James F. Hopewell, *Congregation: Stories and Structure* (Philadelphia: Fortress Press, 1957), 69–71.

7. Heather Murray Elkins © 1990. All rights reserved.

8. David H. Kelsey, *Imagining Redemption* (Louisville: Westminster John Knox Press, 2005).

Chapter 4: STUFF FOR REPAIRING THE WORLD

1. Elizabeth V. Spelman, *Repair: The Impulse to Restore in a Fragile World* (Boston: Beacon Press, 2002).

2. Claude Levi-Straus, *The Savage Mind* (Chicago: University Chicago Press, 1966), 17.

3. John D. Caputo, *On Religion: Thinking in Action* (London and New York: Routledge, 2001), 32.

4. Heather Murray Elkins © 1999. All rights reserved.

5. Heather Murray Elkins © 2000. All rights reserved.

6. Caputo, *On Religion*, 15.

7. Heather Murray Elkins © 2000. All rights reserved.

8. *Daily Christian Advocate*, vol. 5 (Saturday, May 8, 2004), 2238.

9. Ibid., 2339.

10. "A Service of Word and Table IV," *The United Methodist Hymnal* (Nashville: United Methodist Publishing House, 1989), 26.

11. See "News Analysis" and "Confessing Movement Issues Statement on Unity," in *Good News, The Magazine for United Methodist Renewal* 10 (November/December 2005), 32–33, 37.

12. *The United Methodist Book of Worship* (Nashville, Tennessee: United Methodist Publishing House, 1992), 35.

Chapter 5: EVIDENCE OF THINGS NOT SEEN

1. Marcel Proust, *Remembrance of Things Past*, trans. Stephen Hudson, vol. 12, *Time Regained* (London: Chatto and Windus, 1944), 233.

2. Heather Murray Elkins © 2004. All rights reserved.

3. Gordon W, Lathrop, *Holy Things: A Liturgical Theology* (Minneapolis: Augsburg Fortress, 1998), 110.

4. Daniel Marney Elkins, CCQ Murray © 2005. All rights reserved. Music by Ralph Rivers. www.unincorporated.org.

5. John D. Caputo, *On Religion: Thinking in Action* (London and New York: Routledge, 2001), 15.

6. *The United Methodist Book of Worship* (Nashville: United Methodist Publishing House, 1992), 291.

7. Heather Murray Elkins © 2001. All rights reserved.

8. Heather Murray Elkins © 1995. All rights reserved.